WHAT
ABI
TAUGHT
US

AbiH

A MOTHER'S STRUGGLE TO
COME TO TERMS WITH HER
DAUGHTER'S DEATH

WHAT ABI TAUGHT US

LUCY HONE

INCLUDES PRACTICAL STRATEGIES
FOR RESILIENT GRIEVING

ALLEN&UNWIN
SYDNEY · MELBOURNE · AUCKLAND · LONDON

First published in 2016

Allen & Unwin
Level 3, 228 Queen Street
Auckland 1010, New Zealand
Phone: (64 9) 377 3800

Email: info@allenandunwin.com
Web: www.allenandunwin.co.nz

83 Alexander Street
Crows Nest NSW 2065, Australia
Phone: (61 2) 8425 0100

A catalogue record for this book is available
from the National Library of New Zealand

ISBN 978 1 877505 53 9

Internal design by Kate Barraclough
Set in 12.5/17.25 pt Baskerville BT by Bookhouse, Sydney
Printed and bound in Australia by Griffin Press

10 9 8 7 6 5 4 3 2 1

MIX
Paper from
responsible sources
FSC
www.fsc.org
FSC® C009448

The paper in this book is FSC® certified.
FSC® promotes environmentally responsible,
socially beneficial and economically viable
management of the world's forests.

We've got to live, no matter how many skies have fallen.

D.H. Lawrence, *Lady Chatterley's Lover*

• • •

There are so many ways to be brave in this world. Sometimes bravery involves laying down your life for something bigger than yourself, or for someone else. Sometimes it involves giving up everything you have ever known, or everyone you have ever loved, for the sake of something greater. But sometimes it doesn't.

Sometimes it is nothing more than gritting your teeth through pain and the work of every day, the slow walk towards a better life. That is the sort of bravery I must have now.

Veronica Roth, *Allegiant* (Divergent Trilogy)

• • •

Tell me, what is it you plan to do with your one wild and precious life?

Mary Oliver, 'The Summer Day'

Contents

REAPPRAISAL AND RENEWAL

• • •

Foreword

What lies behind us and what lies before us is
nothing compared to what lies within us.

Ralph Waldo Emerson

LUCY WAS A STUDENT of mine in the Master of Applied
Positive Psychology programme at the University of Pennsylvania. We share a deep interest in understanding the nature
of resilience and we share the perspective that resilience is
comprised of an amalgam of abilities, processes, strengths and
core beliefs, which together enable us to adapt, recover and grow
from failure, adversity, even traumatic experiences. At the very
core, we understand that resilience is not armour that protects us
from pain. Rather, resilience enables us to feel pain (and anger,
anxiety, guilt) and to move through these emotions so that we
can continue to feel joy, awe and love. Fundamentally, resilience

is about marshalling what is within us to make it through, and maybe even transform, what is before us.

When I learned of Abi's death, I felt profound sadness and fear: how quickly and permanently our lives can change. I don't know the pain of losing a child but, like many, have experienced loss that feels incomprehensible. Throughout this book, Lucy explores the process of grieving by reflecting on her own experiences and by sharing the research of resilience and mourning. As important, Lucy highlights strategies we can all adopt to exert control over how we negotiate the process of mourning.

Through my own understanding of the resilience process and conversations with people who have lost someone dear, I've come to appreciate a few key principles that are important as we negotiate the path of grieving.

We will find our way. There is not a 'correct' way to grieve, just as there is not a correct way to love. Each of us will discover what helps us and harms us as we work to incorporate the loss into our life. We will likely (perhaps often) feel lost during this discovery, but knowing there is no single path, but rather many different paths that each of us can take, can grant us the freedom to work through the loss in whatever ways feel authentic and helpful.

There are strategies that help. We do not need to be passive in the grieving process. We can influence how we grieve so we do more of what feels productive and less of what is counter-productive. I am not suggesting that healthy mourning rests on a 'can do' spirit. Everyone I have worked with talks about days, hours, maybe just fleeting moments when they 'give in' to whatever it is they are feeling. These moments are as important as those when we feel at the helm.

Many of the strategies that help us deal with the adversities of life can also help us grieve. We can learn resilience by learning how to govern our thoughts, emotions, behaviours, even our physiology. We can develop habits that help us feel gratitude, contentment and joy, without diminishing how desperately we miss our loved one. We can learn how to prevent new fears, anxieties and 'what ifs' from stopping us contributing to and enjoying the life we have. We can learn to manage anger and guilt so these emotions don't close us off from our friends and family. We can take purposeful action, even if some days the action is small, and by taking action we can increase our feelings of mastery and prevent a sense of helplessness from becoming pervasive.

Almost everyone I've spoken with about coping with loss has talked about the sustaining force of their friendships and family. Some people immediately reached out to those they loved; others found it more helpful initially to withdraw into a much smaller and tighter circle; but nearly everyone found they were sustained by the deep and abiding knowledge that they were tethered to other people. At the core of what enables resilience is relationships. When we lose someone, our relationships can take a hit. At the very least, we re-evaluate our relationships and notice the people who are able to be with us during what feels unbearable, as well as the people who are not able to offer what we need. Maybe because we don't all cope the same way; maybe because we are furious at everyone; maybe because loving gets harder when we lose someone—probably for all of these reasons and many more—tending to our relationships following a loss is important, and hard. Resilient strategies can help us keep our relationships strong so we can continue to be sure of each other.

The bottom line is this: we cannot change the past. All we can do is show up for the present and work toward the future we want. Lucy has written a moving book that will help us do just that.

Karen Reivich, PhD
Director of Training Services
Positive Psychology Center
University of Pennsylvania

Chapter 1

The end of the world as we know it

WE WERE DOWN AT Lake Ohau when we first heard of the accident. *An* accident, I should say—that's all it was at the time. We innocently imagined it to be the reason for our daughter and friends' delayed arrival (backed up holiday traffic, closed roads and long diversions maybe?). That scenario was shattered by a policeman calling to say he was on his way to see us.

With those words our world stopped. My memories from then on are sketchy.

What I do remember, distinctly, is that from the moment the policeman confirmed the deaths of our daughter Abi, and of our friends Ella Summerfield and her mother Sally Rumble, I could foresee the mission ahead: this tragedy would challenge us for the rest of our lives. We would miss and mourn all of them, and especially our little girl, every day, forever.

And so it begins, I thought. The road has forked. Welcome to your new life story.

I knew right then I was fighting for survival: the survival of my sanity, my marriage and what was left of our diminished family unit.

Trevor, my husband, our sons Ed (15) and Paddy (14), and I would never be the same family without our Abi. That family had enjoyed many weekends and trips away with our friends, the Summerfields; had had so much fun cycling the Otago Rail Trail two years before; had celebrated New Year's Eve together in the Abel Tasman National Park. Our two families had been utterly entwined since we'd met when the children were at primary school: Ella and Abi the very best of friends; I (and so many others in our small seaside community) adored Sally. They'd been on their way to meet us at Ohau for a weekend biking and walking when another driver sped right through a STOP sign on a rural back road, killing the three of them instantly. Only Sally's husband Shane, who was driving at the time, survived. The magnitude of our loss was unthinkable. To imagine a future without Sally, Ella and Abi in it was utterly absurd.

I wrote this book to offer the bereaved some tools to help them navigate their journey through grief, hoping the strategies I have used to support me in my darkest days might assist others' progression towards acceptance of their loss—and precipitate a return to 'normal' functioning. Whatever normal looks like in worlds that are changed forever.

This was never the life path I anticipated. I won't hesitate to say that it sucks, on so many levels: frequently, profoundly and enduringly. But I often refer back to the poem I read at my mother's funeral 15 years earlier:

• •

To laugh often and love much;
To win the respect of intelligent people and the
    affection of children;
To earn the appreciation of honest critics and
    endure the betrayal of false friends;
To appreciate beauty, to find the best in others;
To leave the world a bit better, whether by a
    healthy child, a garden patch, or a redeemed
    social condition;
To know even one life has breathed easier because
    you have lived.
This is to have succeeded.[1]

• •

If my words can help anyone who is bereaved breathe easier, then that goes some way to making sense out of the senseless and tragically premature deaths of Abi, Ella and Sally.

• • •

The backdrop to this book is resilience psychology. As part of the training for my Master's degree at the University of Pennsylvania in the US, this provided the scientific and theoretical backbone of my practice when our hometown of Christchurch was hit by several large-magnitude earthquakes and thousands of after-shocks between 2010 and 2012. The Canterbury quakes were terrifying to live through—huge shakes, one after another, hitting us without warning and destroying homes, lives and our sense of security. Five times over a 15-month period, our world was turned upside down; the earthquakes killed 185 people (making it the nation's second deadliest natural disaster), wiped out 70 per cent of central Christchurch buildings and left 100,000 homes to be rebuilt. The aftershocks—more than 50 of them measuring above magnitude 5.0 on the Richter scale—were nearly as debilitating. They'd arrive without warning, any time of day or night, putting us permanently on edge for the best part of two years, making us wonder when they would ever stop.

The Canterbury earthquakes gave me my first experience of real fear and personal anxiety, of the heightened levels of psychological arousal that are symptomatic of post-traumatic stress and of the processes required for post-traumatic recovery. The work I did in the aftermath, consulting for various government departments (Ministry of Education, Department of Conservation, NZ LandSars), corporations (Fletcher Earthquake Recovery), community groups and not-for-profits (the Heart Foundation and Mental Health Education Resource Centre) also gave me the opportunity to establish the most effective methods of translating the findings of resilience science so that they might prove useful to ordinary people exposed to real-life traumatic situations. In academic terms, this is known as the translation of evidence to practice. In a nutshell, my work involved educating local people and businesses in the strategies of real-time resilience in a bid to keep them well amid the stresses of living in an earthquake-ravaged city. Dragging scientific research findings out of the ivory towers of academia and translating them into understandable and easily adoptable strategies is what interests me most. It's why I got into academia in the first place.

Armed with an academic understanding of resilience research and the experience of post-traumatic recovery, I suppose I was better placed than most to deal with Abi's death. I knew, for instance, that substantial variation exists in the way people react to adversity, with some individuals managing to bounce back faster than others; that the majority of people are resilient in the face of trauma, and recover to pre-trauma physical and emotional functioning without the need of professional assistance; that certain 'protective factors' have been shown to promote positive responses to trauma; and that parenting styles following significantly stressful life experiences have a substantial impact on children's functioning. I also knew that despite all the fancy scientific methodology and statistical analyses involved in resilience research, study after study indicates that the ingredients of resilience are in fact little more than 'ordinary magic', as Ann Masten, one of the field's leading researchers, likes to refer to them.[2] 'The great surprise of resilience research is the ordinariness of the phenomena,' she explains. 'Resilience appears to be a common phenomenon that results in most cases from the operation of basic human adaptational systems.'

What I wasn't so sure about, at the time of Abi's death, was whether the findings of resilience research applied to bereavement. Would the ordinary processes that Masten and my university teachers talked of help me adapt to this new normal? Could I use this body of evidence and the techniques that had been effective in the post-quake environment to aid my recovery now?

I set out to conduct my own investigation. As a researcher and writer, it seemed logical to keep a diary of my passage through bereavement, so I decided to examine which of the strategies I used in my corporate resilience workshops were effective in combatting the stresses of grieving. In the words of the eminent psychiatrist Dr Viktor Frankl, on his own experience at a prisoner-of-war camp in Nazi Germany, 'both I and my troubles became the object of an interesting psycho-scientific study undertaken by myself'.[3]

In writing this book I want first to acknowledge the wide range of normal reactions to bereavement, including confusion, anger, numbness, frustration, fear, anxiety, relief, jumpiness, sadness and helplessness, to name just a few. For me, in those early days and weeks after Abi's death, so many of these feelings came together it was hard to pinpoint what I was feeling. Mainly numb with shock, I guess. Overwhelmed and helpless, certainly. But it's also important to recognise that some people very quickly develop a hunger for tools to help them cope with grief, and that there is nothing wrong with the desire for action—for what might be called proactive participation in the grieving process.

In this sense, this book is less about what you might experience during bereavement and more about what you might do to enable the process of healthy grieving. There's no escaping the misery and emptiness, but there *are* things you can do that may help you to move through your grief. The tools covered here are designed to empower you at a time of devastating disempowerment. Enabling you to regain a degree of control over your fate and functioning is a central part of the recovery process. This book aims to do just that: to give you some sense of control and action in the face of a helpless situation.

In the chapters ahead I suggest a range of healthy coping strategies, drawn from resilience research and positive psychology, that I hope will assist you in accommodating loss, returning to a 'normal' level of functioning and leading a productive life. Life will never be the same now; it will always be different, with your loss part of your new world and personal identity. But that doesn't mean you won't function effectively and meaningfully again, or fully embrace a life full of love and laughter, alongside plentiful memories of those who once stood beside you. This book aims to help you relearn your world: it offers a jigsaw puzzle of suggested tools designed to help you navigate the grieving process as best you can—without hiding from your feelings or denying the reality, or significance, of your loss.

THIS BOOK IS LESS ABOUT WHAT YOU MIGHT EXPERIENCE AND MORE ABOUT WHAT YOU MIGHT *DO* TO ENABLE THE PROCESS OF HEALTHY GRIEVING.

It is widely accepted among bereavement researchers, counsellors and therapists that there is no universal prescription for grief. We all grieve differently. 'Grief is as individual as your fingerprint,' I recall reading in the bereavement literature given to us by the funeral directors. Skylight, a New Zealand charity, also sent us material about grieving. 'There are no "right" or "wrong" ways to experience grief,' it said. 'There's no secret method that will take your grief instantly away. There are no rules. There is no set timetable. And grief isn't a test, a race or a competition. It might be hard to believe, but it does slowly get easier to handle.'[4]

All of this is sound advice, but there is an undercurrent to the grief literature that I found less helpful—a sense of passivity that is at odds with my own field of academic research. In emphasising the individual nature of grief, bereavement research and the bulk of the literature are currently more focused on the experience of grief (by this I mean the multitude of physical and emotional reactions commonly encountered) and less on strategies aimed at assisting with recovery. This emphasis left me with a feeling that 'anything goes, anything is okay; you just take your time'.

It is certainly true that this approach works for some, but what about those of us who feel we don't have time? What if, like me, you are faced with people who need you to function today, not next month or next year? What then? What if you have a job you love and that contributes substantially to your sense of self-identity? How do you keep that up? What if you have lost a spouse but still have children to function for? Lost a friend but have other friends who need you equally?

This was my situation. I needed to exert whatever control I had left and do anything that was humanly possible to get myself back on my feet as fast as I could. This kind of proactive approach to grieving doesn't mean avoiding grief—I'm not suggesting for a minute anyone can simply side-step grief—nor does it diminish your love for the dead. It just chooses to focus on the living and what you have left. I very quickly understood that, in losing Abi, we'd already lost so much: I was not prepared to lose more. Being there for my family, keeping the remainder together, was the only thing important to me now.

Elisabeth Kübler-Ross's five stages of grief was the only bereavement model I knew about at the time of Abi's death.[5] Based on her research working with terminally ill patients (and devised as a model of *their* common reaction to dying), it is well recognised, and most people seem to be able to name a few of the stages.

While I found it helpful to understand that denial, anger, bargaining, depression and acceptance are frequent reactions to grief, and that 'most people experience these five stages at some point', I found Kübler-Ross's model insufficient for my needs. I wanted to be an active participant in my grieving process, focusing my limited attention and energy on the things I could *do* to support my wellbeing at this vulnerable time. Aware of the statistics (I was told we were now prime candidates for divorce, family estrangement and mental illness), I became determined to *actively* employ all the psychological strategies my traumatised brain could recall to help steer us through the turmoil of those first few days and weeks, let alone the months ahead.

'CHOOSE LIFE, NOT DEATH'. DON'T LOSE WHAT YOU HAVE TO WHAT YOU HAVE LOST.

Talk of five-year recovery timelines for parental bereavement filled me with dread. If Abi's death had taught me anything, it was that life is random and absurdly precious. I had two teenage boys still at home; I could not afford to miss five years. I'd also read the research studies indicating that while the majority of children demonstrate resilience—successfully adapting and recovering to full functioning even when exposed to the most acute forms of trauma and chronic adversities—the biggest threat to those kids was losing their family security and family connections. I vividly recall standing by the oven while a screaming voice inside urged me to 'choose life, not death'. Don't lose what you have to what you have lost.

So began my journey to see if, by deliberately employing strategies known to promote wellbeing and resilience, I could return to normal functioning more quickly. Putting aside all the dreams and hopes for my old life, and focusing on a new goal of 'mainly functioning', I considered what I had learned through my job as a researcher and my practical experience through the quakes that might possibly be useful to us now. When faced with such an extreme reality, could I exert any control, could I actively assist the grieving process, or was I indeed powerless in the face of such overwhelming odds?

My personal journey, over the months since Abi, Ella and Sally died, has convinced me that there is currently very little mainstream awareness of the psychological tools that can assist with grieving. Nobody seems to have applied the wealth of research and proactive psychological techniques from the world of wellbeing and resilience science to this context. George Bonanno, whose work I refer to in this book, is one of the few pioneering researchers pursuing this line of scientific inquiry. However, his findings have yet to have a significant impact on the mainstream public. Ask anyone what they know about grief and loss, and it's the five-stages model, not Bonanno's studies indicating the substantial numbers of resilient grievers, that they'll tell you about.

Fearful of being accused of applying additional pressures on the bereaved, mainstream grief advice maintains its experience-focused stance and its 'anything goes' approach. As a result, most mourners are unaware that there are things they can do that assist the process of healthy bereavement. When wellbeing science has proved that the way we choose to think and the way we choose to act have a substantial influence on our wellbeing, and resilience studies have shown how most people naturally bounce back from all sorts of traumas (including bereavement), it struck me as time to test the effectiveness of my own research field on my personal trauma.

I freely acknowledge that many mourners won't want to adopt a self-help approach to bereavement, but it is also my experience that many do. This book aims to give those people a range of evidence-backed tools to experiment with, to support their gradual return to living fully engaged and meaningful lives.

THE WAY WE CHOOSE TO THINK AND THE WAY WE CHOOSE TO ACT HAVE A SUBSTANTIAL INFLUENCE ON OUR WELLBEING.

Trevor and I agreed from the outset that, if we were going to try to return to normal as quickly as we could, that did not mean we were going into denial. If we did this (went back to work, went out and socialised, carried on with our lives), then we had to promise ourselves that when we felt like shit we'd admit it. We still do. When we want to cry, we will let ourselves. When we want to leave somewhere because staying on seems too futile, we'll get up and go. No questions asked, no explanation required. When we want to stay in bed, we'll do that too.

Throwing yourselves into recovery doesn't mean hiding from grief, pain, misery, aching. It just means you go with the present experience—when these emotions come, you open up to them and let them in—but you choose to get up in the morning and get out in the knowledge that, if you want to win this fight for survival, you've got to step up and take control.

We had no choice in Abi's death, but I believe we do have choices in the way we grieve, and that exerting intentional control over our thoughts and actions helped us weather those terrible first six months, and have continued to be useful as months begin to turn into years. Borrowing again from Viktor Frankl: 'Everything can be taken from a man but one thing: the last of the human freedoms—to choose one's attitude in any given set of circumstances, to choose one's own way.'[6] While my way may not be your way, I have included here the strategies (ways of thinking and acting) that many others have used to nurture their personal resilience in the face of adversity.

Because the passage of time undoubtedly plays its own role in our journey through grief, this book is divided into two parts. Chapters 2–11 concern **Recovery**, and contain strategies I found helpful in the immediate aftermath of the girls' deaths. The remaining chapters focus on **Reappraisal and Renewal** as we start to reassess our lives in the wake of our loss, and consider the myriad ways to honour our loved ones and move forward into the future without them there. Grieving is no linear progression (meaning, you don't start at A and work your way to Z); it's more like an exhausting, frustrating and ghoulish game of Snakes and Ladders (back and forth, up and down). Your grief is unlikely to follow the same progression as mine, so just dip in and out, read back and forth, take your time and find which pieces of grief's jigsaw work for you. The pieces that helped me make sense of this terrible puzzle are brought together in my own Resilient Grieving Model shown in Chapter 17. By all means skip forward and take a look, but it is likely to make more sense once you've read right through.

· ·

She is Gone

Two days after Abi's death, her school held a service so
that the students and our family could gather in the chapel,
united together in our grief. It was a heart-wrenching and
also beautiful service. Our family sat in the front pew,
staring bleakly at Abi's school photo, watching the girls
light candles for her. The principal, Julie Moor, read David
Harkins' poem 'She is Gone',[7] changing the second line to
read 'and' instead of 'or' to reflect that crying and smiling
are equally important and appropriate.

You can shed tears that she is gone
or you can smile because she has lived.

You can close your eyes and pray that she will
    come back
or you can open your eyes and see all that she has left.

Your heart can be empty because you can't see her
or you can be full of the love that you shared.

You can turn your back on tomorrow and live yesterday
or you can be happy for tomorrow because of yesterday.

You can remember her and only that she is gone
or you can cherish her memory and let it live on.

You can cry and close your mind, be empty and turn
    your back
or you can do what she would want: smile, open your
    eyes, love and go on.

D. Harkins, 'Remember Me', 1982.

· ·

CONDUCT YOUR OWN EXPERIMENT— BECOME THE GUINEA PIG

During the writing of this book I have tried to be mindful that everyone's grief experience is different, just as every death is. Every bereavement is governed by multiple factors—our personalities, age, gender, coping styles, faith, grieving history, life experience, as well as the relationship with our dead loved ones and the context of their death. This makes it impossible to prescribe a standard path. I fully acknowledge that there is no one-size-fits-all panacea and that the grief process takes each of us on an individual journey.

In my practice—the training I do with employees and school students to boost their psychological wellbeing and resilience—I always encourage people to try things out for themselves. I'm often asked, how are we supposed to work our way through the raft of research findings and health messages thrown at us when so many of them are conflicting and our own experience seems to buck the trend? In fact, the answer is quite simple: conduct a study on yourself, be your own science experiment. Give the strategies included here a go. Try them out, see what fits with your personality style, and with the environment in which you live and work. Closely monitor whether they are helping your grieving process. If they aren't helping, but are making life harder (perhaps burdening you with another thing to do or think about), then side-step that suggestion and try another.

Nor is it my intention to place expectations (about what should happen, or how you should feel) on those who are grieving. The word *should* has no place in this book: when you lose someone important and grief ensues, no one has the right to tell you how you *should* behave. Rather, this book brings together research and strategies that I (and others) found useful when faced with catastrophic loss—some of which I was aware of prior to Abi's death, some of which I have come across in the months since her death as I struggled for solutions and peace. These are the evidence-based practices that have worked for me, some of which I hope will work for you too.

RECOVERY

Chapter 2

Six strategies for coping in the immediate aftermath

IN THE DAYS FOLLOWING the death of someone you love, plenty of advice will be offered. Among the debilitating symptoms of depression and anxiety, the following strategies were the ones that helped me.

There are no rules—do what *you* need

In the immediate aftermath of the girls' deaths, Trevor and I were very clear that there were no rules we had to follow. As Thomas A. Edison is said to have remarked: 'There are no rules here—we're trying to accomplish something.' When that something is as fundamental as survival, life's normal regulations don't apply. You're in the driver's seat: you're the one who counts, the one who has to survive. You have carte blanche to do whatever it takes for you to get through the first few days and weeks. Sleep all you want, do what you want, feel what you want. No one can tell you how to behave or act.

Even in the first few hours and days after Abi's death, it struck me how important it was that we were accountable only to ourselves—being a bereaved parent is so extreme, it gives you the right to call the shots. With each task we faced, I'd ask myself, 'Is this likely to help us get through this or make things worse?' When trying to decide whether we wanted to go to court to see the driver's trial, we considered whether being there would help our grieving in the long run (because we'll feel we pursued justice), or whether sitting in court, looking at him, hearing him questioned and re-living those 'what if' moments, would make the grieving process harder now and in the future. Viewing our thoughts and actions in this way—asking 'Is this helping or harming?'—is a central tenet of cognitive behavioural therapy and something I'd first come across during my resilience lectures at the University of Pennsylvania. Now I found it a much more useful yardstick by which to evaluate the world than relying on societal conventions. While our attendance in court was expected, it wasn't what we needed. Being there would harm, not help me.

I make this point because I didn't always find it easy to plough my own path; there were times when I knew what society expected of me or what precedent dictated, but I felt compelled to choose a different option. I'm not talking major transgressions but small choices like deciding not to open all the letters of sympathy and support we received each day. Thinking they might offer me comfort further down the track (when I needed to hear fresh recollections of Abi, or even to cement the reality of her death in my mind), I kept some back. Although people might think it rude not to open their letters, I chose, at this time, to put my own needs first and do what was right for me. Along the same lines, I didn't even attempt to write back to all those who sent flowers and cooked food—I sincerely appreciated their help, but writing to each and every one of them would have put more, not fewer demands on myself. Similarly, I have been amazed at how, in the wake of tragic deaths, many bereaved parents and spouses subject themselves to gruelling media interviews which clearly aren't benefiting them in any way. Listen up, people (as Abi would say), no one has the right to interview you in the immediate aftermath, when you are way too raw to think straight. Do it if you want, but just say no if you really don't want to, or you're unsure. There will be plenty of time in the future to comment if you've got things you want to say.

Questioning our thoughts and actions by asking, 'Is this likely to help or harm our recovery?' gave us a modicum of control in a sea of helplessness.

Choose where you focus your attention

Humans have limited processing capacity: our faculties are a long way from infinite.

If I told you that our brains only have about 1500 cubic centimetres of processing capacity, it's not likely to mean much. If we relate that to the fact that scientists estimate we can manage only seven bits of information (that is, differentiating between sounds, visual stimuli, decoding emotions and thoughts) at any one time this may mean a bit more.[1] However, it's still hard to grapple with the implications of such figures for our poor grieving minds. The essential point to understand here is that if even an optimally functioning human brain has limited processing capacity (making selection of the information that we allow into our consciousness vitally important), imagine how much more important selecting the right material is for those of us in mourning. There is no way I would describe my brain as optimally functioning in the days, weeks and even months following Abi's death.

QUESTIONING OUR THOUGHTS AND ACTIONS BY ASKING, 'IS THIS LIKELY TO HELP OR HARM OUR RECOVERY?' GAVE US A MODICUM OF CONTROL IN A SEA OF HELPLESSNESS.

If there is a limit on how much we can experience at any one time, what we choose to focus our attention on becomes extremely influential for determining the content and quality of our daily lives, explains the legendary psychologist, Mihayl Csikszentmihalyi.[2] Understanding this made me realise how important it was for us not to 'waste' our already limited energy and attention on blaming the driver of the car that killed Abi. According to my training, that was non-resilient thinking: it wasn't going to get us anywhere.

Sandy Fox, whose 27-year-old daughter and only child was killed in a hit and run, has a very similar attitude. 'The driver of the van who hit her car was gone in a second, running and running, never found,' she writes in her memoir. 'Friends asked, "Aren't you mad he was never found, so he could be punished?" I thought hard about the answer and finally determined, "No,

I didn't want to have to sit in a courtroom and hear the rehash of what happened and have to look him in the eye and remember his face always." I was much better off emotionally not having to go through that and have any more recurring nightmares than I already had.'[3] Fox chose not to pursue the driver because she felt 'better off emotionally' not having him and his image join her on her grief journey.

I've always thought of the driver as a 'bit part' in our family's tragedy. Csikszentmihalyi's advice that the shape and content of our lives depends on how we direct our limited attention haunted me during the early months. 'Entirely different realities will emerge depending on how it is invested,' he writes.[4] If I was careful about where I focused my attention before Abi's death (imagining it as the beam of a torchlight focused very deliberately in one place), then I was determined not to scatter it mindlessly in this new world where energy was substantially depleted by grief.

THE SHAPE AND CONTENT OF OUR LIVES DEPENDS ON HOW WE DIRECT OUR LIMITED ATTENTION.

Remembering you are in control of where you choose to focus your attention in life (and that your capacity for processing the outer world is limited) is an especially powerful tool during bereavement. You choose what you focus the torch beam of your personal attention on. It is not up to your parents, your friends, the media, solicitors, terrorists, drivers, or even victim support workers. To repeat Karen Reivich's message to me soon after the girls' deaths, resilience is 'more a matter of making it your intention to put your attention here rather than there'.[5]

YOU WILL NOT HAVE MY HATRED

In November 2015, Parisian Antoine Leiris gave the world a supreme demonstration of our power to select the focus of our attention. In a Facebook post called 'You will not have my hatred', after terrorist attacks in Paris in December robbed him of his wife, he wrote:

Friday night you stole the life of an exceptional being, the love of my life, the mother of my son, but you will not have my hatred. I do not know who you are and I don't want to know, you are dead souls. If the God for which you kill indiscriminately made us in his image, each bullet in the body of my wife will have been a wound in his heart.

Therefore I will not give you the gift of hating you. You have obviously sought it but responding to hatred with anger would be to give in to the same ignorance that has made you what you are. You want me to be afraid, to cast a mistrustful eye over my fellow citizens, to sacrifice my freedom for security. Lost. Same player, same game.

I saw her this morning. Finally, after many nights and days of waiting. She was just as beautiful as when she left on Friday evening, as beautiful as when I fell madly in love with her more than 12 years ago. Of course I'm devastated with grief, I will give you that tiny victory, but it will be a short-term grief. I know she will join us every day and that we will find each other again in a paradise of free souls which you will never have access to.

We are only two, my son and I, but we are more powerful than all the armies of the world. In any case, I have no more time to waste on you, I need to get back to Melvil who is waking from his afternoon nap. He's just 17 months old; he'll eat his snack like every day, and then we are going to play like we do every day; and every day of his life this little boy will insult you with his happiness and freedom. Because, no, you won't have his hatred either.

A. Leiris, 'You will not have my hatred',
Facebook post, 17 November 2015.

Take your time

The morning after Abi died, the boys' school chaplain Bosco Peters and his wife Helen arrived at our house. I think I was vaguely aware that Bosco's daughter had been killed in a devastating accident, but I remember being too shy to ask—in case it was the wrong thing to do. On that Sunday, he and Helen came and sat with us, and others, in our sitting room. We drank tea and talked. They shared their miserable and painful journey through five years of grief for Catherine, and gave us some very good advice. 'Don't rush, take your time, there is no hurry to do anything these next few days,' Bosco said. 'Take your time with Abi, and don't rush into having the funeral before you are ready. There is time.'

I have been so grateful for the hard-earned wisdom of those who have been there before us. They know how much time there is to mourn the dead once they are truly gone—either buried or cremated. Abi died on the Saturday and came home from the funeral director's on the Wednesday. Thanks to Bosco's advice, we had five precious days to spend with her before the funeral the following Monday.

That time at home with her body was a game changer for me, and for my grief. It's one of those time-honoured rituals that have substantially helped (for other rituals see Chapter 18). I know it was important for others too. I recently copied a text from my dear friend Kimberley, whose son Henry was one of Abi's and Ella's closest friends, as a concrete reminder of the importance of having her home and spending time with her. 'Thank you for always sharing Abi with us. Yesterday was beautiful, we all feel calmer having said our goodbyes. I hope sitting with your girl today gives you comfort. For strength, you can lean on us for as long as it takes.'[6]

Feel the pain: walk right in, feel it and weep

A friend from my Master's programme contacted me a few weeks after Abi's death, offering me a bit of 'Pema wisdom'. She was referring to the American Buddhist teacher and author, Pema Chödrön, of whom I'd never heard. While acknowledging that the moments when our lives fall apart are a test, Chödrön urges us to regard these as a normal part of our unfolding life. 'We think that the point is to pass the test or to overcome the problem, but the truth is that things don't really get solved. They come together and they fall apart. Then they come together again and fall apart again. It's just like that,' she writes. So, this is just the way life is. Just like that. The answer to living in a world where there are no constants is, says Chödrön, to allow room for all this to happen, accept that change will occur, that life contains much suffering, and to allow 'room for grief, for relief, for misery, for joy'.[7]

26

This struck a sufficient chord for me to read the rest of her book, *When Things Fall Apart: Heart advice for difficult times*, and to discover that much of Buddhist thinking is really useful for those of us experiencing substantial loss. Wandering the pages of Chödrön's prose shifted my perspective and helped calm the voice of outrage inside me. Chödrön suggests that experiencing loss and difficult times is standard in the course of a life, and that we have a choice in the way we react. When traumatic events happen, we have a natural tendency to run from the hurt, but Chödrön advises us to walk straight into it, to approach the pain, loss, envy and longing head on. 'Most of us do not take these situations as teachings. We automatically hate them. We run like crazy. We use all kinds of ways to escape—all addictions stem from this moment when we meet our edge and we just can't stand it.'[8]

WALK STRAIGHT INTO IT; APPROACH THE PAIN, LOSS, ENVY AND LONGING HEAD ON.

Those words echo exactly my own experience particularly in those first few days and weeks following the girls' deaths. I felt we'd somehow been instantly propelled from the life we knew, with all its comforts, routines, expectations and trivial complications, to a different realm of existence. Enduring such traumatic events put us 'out there on the edges of life', was how I used to think of it, picturing us on the outer rings of Saturn, quite separate from the world as we'd known it and which steadfastly continued to spin over there in the distance. Even amid such despair and so early after their deaths, however, I could also see there was a clarity to this life, a richness of experience that is rarely encountered in everyday existence.

Watching children visit Abi as she lay in her open, low-sided coffin—surrounded by the familiarity and comforts of her own room, listening to them chatting to her, their open, honest, heartfelt, raw communication—I knew we were seeing love and compassion at a level far beyond that of our usual, mundane experience. Through the pain, beauty and love shone. We didn't attempt to shield ourselves from it. Instead, we leaned right in.

Now familiar with Worden's Four Tasks of Mourning (see Chapter 4), I can relate this experience to his second task: that of processing the pain of grief. 'Not everyone experiences the same intensity of pain or feels it in the same way,' he writes, 'but it is nearly impossible to lose someone to whom you have been deeply attached without experiencing some level of pain. The newly bereaved are often unprepared to deal with the sheer force and nature of emotions that follow a loss.'[9]

Trevor and I are lucky that we share a similar approach to emotions: both naturally open to feeling and expressing our emotions, we find it relatively easy to share how we feel with those around us. Twenty-five years ago, when I first met him, his forthright nature, honesty and openness were among the things that appealed to me most. And his kindness. Little did I know that these would be the things that united us in our darkest days. Feeling pain and sorrow—sobbing loudly and weeping silently—are scary things, but in the end I came to realise that when I hurt so much already, experiencing the full brunt of these emotions could in no way hurt me more. Experiencing pain is just part of living, a symptom of the love we have for those we have lost.

Beware of the grief 'ambush'

In their book, *I Wasn't Ready to Say Goodbye: Surviving, coping and healing after the sudden death of a loved one*, Brook Noel and Pamela Blair introduce the notion of the grief 'ambush'.[10] I found myself ambushed by grief again only very recently, when visiting our new supermarket. It had been destroyed in the quakes, and was at last being reopened after almost five years. Our whole community had been eagerly awaiting the official opening, all laughing about how ridiculous it was to be so excited about a new supermarket. But five years is a long time and we live a fair distance from the city centre, on a peninsula with only one road in, one road out. Opening day finally came, and I raced into the car park, bright eyed, bushy tailed, thrilled to have some decent groceries on our doorstep at long last. I parked the car—and, as I was getting out, grief overwhelmed me. Suddenly and unexpectedly filled with memories of all the times I'd visited the supermarket with Abi, first as a toddler and then as a school girl, the tears began to flow. And there was no stopping them. The whole journey round the supermarket was the same: I could not stop myself crying, acutely aware of how much our lives had changed since 2011 when I had last stood on the same spot. Abi was just eight years old then, so never far from my side. As a little girl we'd buy her ham from the deli counter and eat it as we pushed the trolley around. Now, here I was living such a different life, looking back to a time when her death would have been unimaginable. Thankfully, I saw one of Abi's friends and her dad, had a quick cry on them in the Coke aisle, and then powered on, taking refuge behind my sunglasses once more.

Grief ambushes are a normal part of bereavement but, arriving unannounced, they sure can make you feel silly.

No one strategy will prepare you for these moments, but having a name for them helps us understand what's happening, and so they derail us less. Knowing there will be times when you are blindsided with grief—that misery will overwhelm you at the most unexpected and often inappropriate moments and places—puts you in a better position to weather the grief ambush when it next happens.

Re-establish routines

In Christchurch's post-quake environment, I learned of the importance of re-establishing routines to counteract the negative effects of trauma. The need to re-establish normal routines as quickly as is humanly and physically possible is recognised by disaster researchers as an important initial step towards recovery. Authorities talk about establishing 'normalisation'—that is, getting kids back to schools, parents back to work, enabling social lives, churches, clubs, leisure facilities and communities to resume functioning. They acknowledge the importance of regarding this as the 'new normal'.

Re-establishing routines tells our brains that we are safe, that the crisis period is over, and it's okay to disarm the red-alert functioning that is our bodies' reaction to traumatic events. The predictability of routines helps us feel safer, and minimises stress, anxiety and hopelessness.

Studies show that family resilience really matters: keeping the family together after a disaster, resuming routines and ordinary functioning as best you can, helps the children cope. Returning to the childcare centre, going back to school, to family meals, bedtime stories, sports clubs and opportunities to socialise all give us a feeling that the chaos is over and life is (gradually) adopting a new normal. These repetitive actions are reassuring not only to children but also to adults around them.

With 16- and 14-year-old boys in the house, I was aware that they needed to experience as much normality as possible to help their brains recover from the trauma and to carry on without Abi around. That's not to say we didn't grieve openly at home. We did, we still do. But getting them back to school gave us structure to work with. I was surprised how much they wanted to do this, and how quickly. Within a fortnight, they were both back at school and happier for it.

THE PREDICTABILITY OF ROUTINES HELPS US FEEL SAFER, AND MINIMISES STRESS, ANXIETY AND HOPELESSNESS.

It took Trevor and me longer to get ourselves back to work. In those first few weeks after Abi's death we stumbled around, struggling to pay attention to anything for very long, with wandering focus and only sporadic and minimal interest in the activities that usually filled our lives. Looking back, I have mental pictures of us occupying our days, always starting with a long walk with the dog, sometimes crying for the majority of it, sometimes numb and silent, at other times chewing our feelings over and over, trying to work it out, as if there was a solution to be found if we could only think it through hard enough, talk it over long enough. But while we couldn't get ourselves back to work, re-establishing meal times, and the regular routine of exercise, dog walk, coffee, breakfast, chores, lunch, chores, nap, dinner, TV and bed helped. At around the six weeks mark, we went back to work. Trevor returned to his building company, which his crew had valiantly continued to operate without him. I was desperate to resume my research and adamant that I wasn't going to let my current PhD projects go. I talked to my colleagues, and we agreed I'd start with an hour or two and see how it went. Oddly, it was a tremendous relief to focus my mind elsewhere and I was encouraged by how much my poor smashed-up brain could manage. With exceedingly low expectations, the pressure was minimal and gradually my hours picked up. Work has been a welcome distraction and provided me with a lifeline of routine ever since.

I recently met with another woman, Anna, who had just lost her twin sister in a plane crash. I was full of admiration on the morning I met up with her —just three weeks after her sister's death—as she battled to hold back her tears, get the kids out the door and head off to work. Getting back into the classroom where she works as a teaching assistant helps, she said. Being absorbed by the children's activities gives her a much-needed rest from grieving, at least for that part of the day. Seeing the kids carry on as normal tells her brain that normal still exists, that life carries on, that the immediate threat is over. More than anything, short bouts of work provide us with a welcome rest and temporary refuge from grieving.

Chapter 3

What can resilience psychology teach us about grieving?

WHILE THE FIELD OF psychology has traditionally focused on risk factors (predictors of undesirable life outcomes), I am one of a growing breed of academic researchers focused on protective factors that have been shown to promote wellbeing and assist with recovery among people facing trauma, stress and adversity. Bereavement research remains primarily focused on unpacking the complexities of the bereavement experience (identifying the different stages we go through) and on the alleviation of grief's negative emotional consequences—anxiety and depression. So when we lost Abi, and my reading on bereavement began, I was struck by how little these two fields of research had crossed over. While resilience psychologists have unearthed all sorts of findings about how to assist people in bouncing back from trauma, bereavement research (and the corresponding literature handed out to people like you and me) featured few of these strategies. I had lived through trauma—the series of earthquakes that rocked my city from 2010–2012—and previously grieved my mother, so it struck me that the tools we advocate for promoting resilience might well be useful during bereavement. The American Psychological Association defines resilience as 'the process of adapting well in the face of adversity, trauma, tragedy [and] threats'.[1] It seems to me there's sufficient trauma and tragedy in grief to make this body of research relevant.

For instance, resilience research highlights the immensely positive difference that close family ties, social support, family routines, parenting quality, thinking and coping styles (such as optimism and positive emotions), physical activity, and cultural and spiritual beliefs can have on human reaction to adversity. There's no doubt individual personality differences also play a big role in how people react; some people cope well with stress, some are more stress reactive. But, by studying those who have displayed resilience in the face of extreme adversity, researchers have demonstrated that something of a blueprint for resilience does exist. Their findings make for fascinating reading.

For example, having studied the genetic, psychological, biological, social and spiritual factors behind the resilience of prisoners of war, Special Forces instructors, and ordinary men and women who have endured harrowing traumas and gone on to thrive, Steven Southwick (Professor of Psychiatry, Post-Traumatic Stress Disorder and Resilience at Yale Medical School) and his colleague Dr Dennis Charney (Professor of

Psychiatry and Neuroscience at the Mount Sinai School of Medicine) were astonished to discover that while genes do play a role in individual levels of resilience, they are only part of the story. 'When we began our study, we assumed that resilience was rare and resilient people were somehow special, perhaps genetically gifted. It turns out, we were wrong. Resilience is common and can be witnessed all around us. Even better, we learned that everyone can learn and train to be more resilient. The key involves knowing how to harness stress and use it to our advantage.'[2]

For one of their studies, Southwick and Charney interviewed 30 former prisoners of war from the infamous Hanoi Hilton camp in Vietnam, selecting those who had coped with six to eight years of imprisonment and gone on to lead successful and meaningful lives. 'We were particularly interested to discover how they handled the trauma and stress of being a prisoner of war 8000 miles away from home and come out the other end and be a strong person,' Charney explained in a subsequent interview.[3] They found that, despite being held in solitary confinement for years and physically tortured, several common factors emerged as critical for survival. One was continued support from other prisoners. By developing what the prisoners referred to as a 'tap code', neighbouring men were able to maintain communications with one another by tapping their way through the alphabet; they were never totally isolated and could still support each other. 'Everybody needs a tap code to get through tough times, very few can go it alone,' says Charney, explaining how friendships support us.

Among these prisoners, other common ways of coping were humour, faith and spirituality, the presence of role models, a willingness to help others and an optimistic outlook. The POWs also worked hard to maintain physical fitness, despite the limitations of their cells. This, said the researchers, boosted their self-esteem and mental toughness.

I'd first come across Charney's work and the notion and practice of resilience training at the University of Pennsylvania, where our lead instructor on the topic was Karen Reivich. Co-director of the Penn Resiliency Project, Reivich had several years of experience developing resilience training programmes for schools and corporate organisations, and had been awarded the contract to train the entire US Army in the psychological skills of resilience, making them as psychologically fit as they were physically fit. She taught me three fundamental truths about resilience: 1) most people are resilient; 2) resilience requires very ordinary processes; and 3) these processes can be taught and learned.

Later, after Abi died, she wrote to me: 'So many of the interventions I teach are not exactly rocket science . . . More a matter of making it your intention to put your attention here rather than there.'[4] Her words gave me hope. I reckoned I could choose to put my attention on the good things I still had in life, on nurturing the relationships with those close to me, on accepting what I could change and what I could not, on using my strengths to assist with recovery.

This book therefore looks at the types of personal assets and resources (promotive and protective factors in psychological terms) that have been shown to predict good outcomes in resilience studies, and examines their usefulness in a new context—that of grieving. It also asks a number of questions. What helps people cope during bereavement? Do some people manage to recover faster than others? Which ways of acting and thinking help us get through the loss of a loved one, and which hold us back? How long does grief have to last: is there a fixed time frame? Is it possible to grieve too quickly and is that a sign of denial? Does it all come down to individual differences, or might some of these strategies prove helpful for numerous people going through grief?

'SO MANY OF THE INTERVENTIONS I TEACH ARE NOT EXACTLY ROCKET SCIENCE . . . MORE A MATTER OF MAKING IT YOUR INTENTION TO PUT YOUR ATTENTION HERE RATHER THAN THERE.' KAREN REIVICH

I must confess that when I first started writing this book I was sceptical (even within myself) about the notion of resilient grieving—was it really possible to expedite the grief process by employing certain cognitive and behavioural strategies? Were the evidence-based tools we use in resilience training useful in the context of bereavement? Or was I deluded, heading for a fall? Was I, in fact, just demonstrating one of Kübler-Ross's famous five stages of grief—that of denial? I hesitated and pondered, but my understanding of humans' extraordinary capacity to bounce back from a wide range of traumas (natural disasters, war, imprisonment) convinced me to try. Who was to say that the same resilience skills and recovery strategies cannot be applied to life after loss?

Then I found George Bonanno and a new breed of research academics, all of whom are starting to explore what resilience looks like in the context of bereavement. Similarly, Thomas Attig assured me that while our initial reactions to grief are passive and somewhat beyond our control, we are not entirely helpless in grief: grieving is in fact filled with choice.[5] These researchers' findings, gathered via structured interviews, and cross-sectional and longitudinal survey data, were compelling.

Over the course of 20 years of research, Bonanno, a clinical psychologist at Columbia University and author of *The Other Side of Sadness: What the new science of bereavement tells us about life after loss*, has discovered that coping well in the face of bereavement is much more common than bereavement researchers have previously reported. His studies show that most people bounce back from bereavement in much the same way they do from other adverse life experiences (child poverty, war, natural disasters, terrorism).

His studies also confirm that there is a resilient type of person. 'We consistently find specific psychological characteristics among people who cope well during bereavement. One such characteristic is the ability to adjust to the shifting demands of different situations. This is a kind of behavioural flexibility . . . Every stress and adversity challenges us in particular ways. The types of struggles people confront when they lose a loved one to a graphic or violent death are different from the stresses that arise when a loved one succumbs to a prolonged illness. Dealing with loss is different from coping with other types of violent or dangerous trauma, like surviving a hurricane or tsunami. By and large, the people who deal best with these different situations are those who can do what it takes to get through the event.'[6]

Those words sum up my attitude to resilience and surviving bereavement—for me, it's been a matter of doing what I can to get through each hour, day, week, month and year. That's the mission synopsis right there.

By applying the same mixed-method scientific methodology that the likes of Masten, Southwick and Charney, and Reivich have applied to other types of trauma, Bonanno and his colleagues have challenged some of the traditional myths about bereavement. For example, grief experts had previously assumed that expressing emotional pain was an essential part of bereavement; that anyone not doing so (which they term *absent grief*) was demonstrating denial, and that the failure to express this pain would result in what they termed a *delayed grief reaction* further down the track.

IT'S BEEN A MATTER OF DOING WHAT I CAN TO GET THROUGH EACH HOUR, DAY, WEEK, MONTH AND YEAR.

One of Bonanno's research team's most consistent findings is that we don't all have to travel through the various stages of grief; nor do we have to necessarily *work through* several tasks of mourning, as many grief theorists have suggested. Furthermore, there is no robust scientific study that has demonstrated the existence of delayed grief. They found 'people who were well adjusted after a loss were almost always healthy years later. Delayed grief simply did not occur.'[7] This provided me with a vitally important piece in my own jigsaw puzzle of grief.

Similarly, Bonanno's findings on the concept of 'grief work' (a phrase originally coined by Sigmund Freud in 1917 and picked up by Erich Lindemann in the 1940s) exposed the limitations of that theory. 'As researchers began to devote more attention to the bereavement process . . . it became apparent that, despite the near unanimity with which mental health professionals endorsed the grief work perspective, there was a surprising lack of empirical support for such a view,' he explained in 2004.[8] Instead, Bonanno and his colleagues suggest there are three common responses to bereavement: some bereaved individuals experience *chronic grief* (the loss overwhelms them and they seriously struggle, sometimes for years, to return to normal functioning); some experience a gradual *recovery* (having initially suffered and displayed symptoms of depression or post-traumatic stress disorder, they gradually, over several months, return to pre-event functioning); but most individuals are resilient in the face of grief in that they maintain relatively stable, healthy levels of psychological and physical functioning. Resilient individuals may experience several weeks of sporadic preoccupation or restless sleep but they 'generally exhibit a stable trajectory of healthy functioning across time, as well as the capacity for generative experiences and positive emotions'.[9]

Because bereavement research has historically been dominated by studies involving individuals experiencing acute and chronic grief (known among health professionals as 'complicated grief'), such reactions came to be regarded as the norm. 'Bereavement theorists have been highly sceptical about individuals who do not show pronounced distress reactions or who display positive emotions following loss, assuming that such individuals are rare and suffer from pathological or dysfunctional forms of absent grief,' writes Bonanno. In fact, having reviewed all the available research, his studies show that 'the vast majority' maintain healthy functioning. For example, several different studies following bereaved individuals over time have estimated that chronic grief occurs in just 10–15 per cent of individuals,[10] whereas bereaved individuals demonstrating resilience (relatively low levels of depression or distress) have consistently approached or exceeded 50 per cent of the sample,[11] and 60 per cent of bereaved study participants have consistently reported high life satisfaction over the years.[12]

This is not to say that any of us is immune to grief. I still have afternoons when all I can do is retreat to bed and let myself go in the knowledge that having to cope with Abi's loss is not okay. It's not okay that we have to endure this, and it's not okay that she had to die and miss all the wonderful moments of her life—or even the crappy ones too. One single moment of motorised madness should not have robbed our beautiful girls of decades of living. That's simply not right or fair. But I'm not angry—I don't see the point. Mostly, I still function and, I'm willing to admit, this is something of a relief. I'm surprised how quickly Trevor, the boys and I have managed to bounce back from the trauma of Abi's sudden and utterly unexpected death, and how readily we've managed to juggle sadness and continued living, and mostly maintained full psychological and physical functioning. Even after the death of a child. Discovering that there are plenty of others like us has made me feel less as if we're unfeeling or freakish. Reading accounts of resilient grievers who have continued to suffer negative emotions, misery and longing for their loved ones, but done so while carrying on with full and rewarding lives, somehow makes it feel more okay to act this way.

Because it's so important, I'm going to repeat this one more time. Studies show most people make a good recovery from the psychological and social effects of significant disasters, including bereavement. They also show resilience requires very ordinary processes. Karen Reivich describes these processes as a stew, containing lots of different ingredients, some of which we will have in plentiful supply, some we may be running low on. We may not like the taste of some of them; others will immediately appeal to us. I like to think of it as a jigsaw puzzle, but, ultimately, it's up to us to find the things that help us process what's happened and relearn how to live in the world we are faced with.

10 TOOLS TO BUILD RESILIENCE

Dennis Charney and Steve Southwick are among the leading world experts in the neurobiology and treatment of mood and anxiety disorders, as well as the neurobiology of resilience to stress. They have found that psychological stress alters brain functions; certain identified key factors are related to resilience; and it is very possible to train yourself to be more resilient. They have identified the following 10 tools for promoting resilience.

1. Adopt a positive attitude:
   - Optimism is strongly related to resilience ('sounds trivial, but it's really hard').
   - Optimism is in part genetic ('but genes are not destiny and you can make yourself more optimistic').
   - Optimism can be learned (via tools such as cognitive behavioural therapy).
   - Unbridled and unrealistic optimism (aka 'Pollyanna optimism') is not good and gets you in trouble.
   - A truly optimistic person confronts the brutal facts of their current reality, accurately appraises the trauma and situation, but simultaneously has the confidence that they will prevail in the end, regardless of the difficulties.

2. Think flexibly:

- Cognitive flexibility through cognitive reappraisal is strongly related to resilience.
- Traumatic experiences can be re-evaluated by altering the event's perceived value and meaningfulness.
- Benefits can be derived from stress and trauma: it is possible to reframe, assimilate, accept and recover; these skills can be learned.
- Failure is an essential ingredient for growth.

3. Embrace a personal moral compass:

- Developing a set of core beliefs that very few things can shatter is strongly related to resilience.
- For many this takes the form of faith in conjunction with strong religious and/or spiritual beliefs, but it doesn't have to be so.
- Altruism (giving to others) has been strongly related to resilience.
- Having a survivor's mission is also strongly related.

4. Find a resilient role model:

- Role models are important; they can be found in your own life but you don't have to know them (e.g. Viktor Frankl, Nelson Mandela).
- Imitation is a very powerful mode of learning.

5. Face your fears:

- Fear is a normal part of life and can be used as a guide; facing your fears can increase your self-esteem.
- Learn and practise skills necessary to move through fear.

6. Develop active coping skills:
   - Resilient individuals use active, rather than passive, coping skills.
   - Minimise your appraisal of the stressor, create positive statements about yourself, and actively seek support from others.

7. Establish and nurture a supportive social network:
   - Very few can 'go it alone'; humans need a safety net during times of stress.
   - Develop your own kind of 'tap code'.
   - Considerable emotional strength accrues from close relationships with people and organisations.

8. Attend to physical wellbeing:
   - Physical exercise has positive effects on physical hardiness, mood, and improves self-esteem.

9. Train regularly and rigorously in multiple areas:
   - Change requires systematic and disciplined activity.
   - Concentrate on training in multiple areas: emotional intelligence, moral integrity, physical endurance.

10. Recognise, utilise and foster signature strengths:
    - Learn to recognise your character strengths and engage them to deal with difficult and stressful situations.

Adapted from D. Charney, 'The Resilience Prescription'.[13]

Chapter 4

Accept the loss has occurred

FIVE SHORT WORDS—ACCEPT THE loss has occurred: so easy to write, so hard to do. I wrote the title of this chapter and then just stared at the words for an eternity. How can I tell you simply to 'accept the loss has occurred', when it is the greatest challenge of all?

Accepting that the loss has occurred is recognised by many bereavement researchers, grief counsellors and therapists as an essential step in successful grieving. William Worden, co-principal investigator for Harvard's Child Bereavement Study, and whose book, *Grief Counseling and Grief Therapy: A handbook for the mental health practitioner,* is viewed by many as the bible for complicated grief, regards accepting the reality of the loss as one of the essential tasks of mourning. The others are to process grief's pain; to adjust to a world without the deceased; and to find an enduring connection with the deceased while simultaneously embracing a new life. All of these would become familiar to me in time, but accepting the reality of the loss was the first step.

After Abi died, we worked very hard on accepting as quickly as we could that this terrible thing had happened. That was my way: I regarded accepting the loss as the first step, not out of knowledge of any particular grief theory, but intuitively. It was my logical first big step in survival. This doesn't mean it will be your first step. For some it's plainly obvious; for others it takes time. But, accepting the loss has occurred is a necessary step in adapting to it. Accept that it is irreversible: that no amount of wishing, wanting, urging or bargaining will change the outcome. This terrible thing has happened, I told myself over and over. To me, to us, to her. She is Dead. It is Done. And there's nothing I can do.

I remember the discussion Trevor and I had one week after the girls died. We sat on the rocky wall, just above the beach, and looked out to sea, wondering what to do, what to say, how to go on living in our hateful, hopeless new world.

It wouldn't have been any different if she'd died of cancer, I said to him. We'd be in just the same place right now, bereft and full of desolate, profound and overwhelming sadness. In fact, we could argue, that would have been worse. Watching her die, willing her to live, hanging on to hope and watching it slip away—I wouldn't choose that.

But then I wouldn't choose this—the sudden, abrupt wrenching of life—either.

That's the point, though. In death there is no choice. Death doesn't discriminate between good and bad, young and old, rich and poor. It is entirely random. We don't get to choose between sudden or slow, nor when it occurs, nor how.

And in my mind, pondering why, or how, was a waste of precious energy, which was suddenly in very short supply. That was energy we were going to need to get through each day, to maintain the uphill struggle for the weeks, months and no doubt years to come. So, taking Reivich's words literally, I decided not to focus my attention on the mechanisms of their deaths—how Abi, Ella and Sally died, or, for that matter, how their deaths might have been avoided. Right now, accepting the loss had occurred, and that we *had to* move forward throughout the rest of our lives without Abi, was going to require every ounce of energy we would have left. I'm fortunate that Trevor could do the same.

DEATH DOESN'T DISCRIMINATE BETWEEN GOOD AND BAD, YOUNG AND OLD, RICH AND POOR. IT IS ENTIRELY RANDOM.

Very occasionally I've had to stop myself from heading down the 'what ifs' rabbit warren. Researchers call this very common practice 'bargaining'. What if we hadn't received the phone call offering her a ride that day? What if I'd stopped her from going? What if I hadn't planned that weekend away at Ohau? What if I had never wanted to go bloody mountain biking and we had just stayed at home (as Ed and Trevor wanted)? What if anything had delayed them even just for a second? Usually, I'll get this far, mostly just two questions in, before the futility strikes me. 'What ifs' are pointless, irrelevant and, above all, cruel. Stop questioning why: there are no answers. They eat up vital energy on a fruitless endeavour. There were a thousand opportunities for there to have been a different outcome from that car journey, a different end to that fateful day, but none of them eventuated. Their deaths are real. The accident really happened. Those three beautiful girls are not coming back to us again. Ever. Get this fact into your thick skull as quickly as you can, I told myself. Do not waste time, or energy, wondering what could have happened differently. What's happened has happened. Get on with it, accept they have gone, and work out a way of dealing with that reality so that it doesn't cost you the rest of your family life.

ACCEPTING THE LOSS AS REAL AND UNCHANGEABLE IS A VITAL PART OF LEARNING TO LIVE WITH THAT LOSS AND MANAGING THE LOSS EXPERIENCE.

It's not a question of *getting over* it. I don't want to get over Abi—successful adaptation does not include pushing her out of our lives. She may not be here with us physically but I am well aware that she will forever be part of me. I am suggesting, however, that accepting the loss as real and unchangeable is a vital part of learning to live with that loss and with the loss experience. I'm also suggesting that (for some of us at least) this is something we can exert some control over. Trevor and I have determinedly refused to play the 'what if' game. Most of the time we have been successful. No, Elisabeth Kübler-Ross, we will not participate in your bargaining stage. Nor will I feel anger. No amount of either will bring our daughter back. Abi is gone. She was killed in a car crash. She's never walking down our steps and through our front door again. Accepting her enormous (and hideously abrupt) absence from our lives is, for me, the first stage in learning to live in this brave new world that I don't like very much. Bereavement researcher, Thomas Attig agrees this is the best approach: 'Accepting the reality of death and suffering can only be the beginning point of effective grieving response, not the end.'[1]

And try to understand

Three days after Abi died, a family friend messaged me on Facebook to share an adapted version of Edgar Guest's poem, 'A Child of Mine'. Our eldest, Ed, read this, the female version, at Abi's funeral.

• •

A Child of Mine

I will lend you, for a little time,
A child of mine, He said.
For you to love the while she lives,
And mourn for when she's dead.
It may be six or seven years,
Or twenty-two or three.
But will you, till I call her back,
Take care of her for Me?
She'll bring her charms to gladden you,
And should her stay be brief.
You'll have her lovely memories,
As solace for your grief.

I cannot promise she will stay,
Since all from earth return.

But there are lessons taught down there,
I want this child to learn.
I've looked the wide world over,
In search for teachers true.
And from the throngs that crowd life's lanes,
I have selected you.
Now will you give her all your love,
Nor think the labour vain.
Nor hate me when I come to call
And take her back again?

I fancied that I heard them say,
Dear Lord, Thy will be done!
For all the joys Thy child shall bring,
The risk of grief we'll run.
We'll shelter her with tenderness,
We'll love her while we may,
And for all the happiness we have known,
Forever grateful stay.
But should the angels call for her,
Much sooner than we've planned.
We'll brave the bitter grief that comes,
And try to understand.

'A Child of Mine', adapted from Edgar Albert Guest who wrote the
original version for a male child, circa 1930.

• •

I loved this poem from the moment I first read it. It's curious how poetry can sometimes fill the void, expressing the right thing in a way that somehow fits. Helping the senseless make sense, lending some structure to chaos, backed by the reassurance and order of its predictive iambic pentameter. I love that it singles us out from the throngs, reminding us that we were fortunate to have been Abi's keepers. I respect its reminder not to think the labour—all we did for her across those years—was in vain. And I hang on to the thousands of memories as 'solace for my grief'. As a poem, it fits.

As time has gone by, however, it is the first and last sentences that I return to time and time again. I will lend you, for a little time, a child of mine, he said. For you to love the while she lives and mourn for when she'd dead, but should the angels call for her, much sooner than we've planned, we'll brave the bitter grief that comes, and try to understand.

That's what I do: try to understand. Again, and again and again, we try to understand. It's not like I wrangle with the hows and whys of how it happened—I won't let myself do that—but hardly a day goes by when those four words don't enter my head as I perpetually try to understand that it did happen. As I try to grapple with her loss, the emptiness, the longing, the confusion and disbelief. Come on, brain, I urge, get on with it, catch up. But it takes time, this grieving, and I know the process cannot be hurried.

Death challenges our assumptions about the world we live in and the life we lead. Bereavement invokes serious questions. What was the purpose of her life? How can I go on living normally in this world when I know such terrible things can happen at any time? What's life all about? Trying to understand, making sense of it all, is recognised by psychologists as central to the grieving process. The battle for acceptance is a tough one.

Chapter 5

Humans are hard wired to cope

GRIEF IS A NORMAL and natural emotional reaction to the loss of a loved one, and cannot be avoided. It involves misery and anguish and suffering, no doubt about that. But, does it necessarily have to derail us entirely and chronically? Haven't we, as humans, had to deal with death throughout history? Isn't coping with bereavement in fact one of the fundamental skills of human existence? Almost 18 months after Abi's death, I came to think so.

George Bonanno's research has demonstrated that, if you talk to lots of people experiencing grief, rather than confining research to those experiencing prolonged or complicated grief, then coping with death is actually quite normal. 'Above all, [bereavement] is a human experience. It is something we are wired for, and it is certainly not meant to overwhelm us. Rather, our reactions to grief seem designed to help us accept and accommodate losses relatively quickly so that we can continue to live productive lives. Resilience doesn't mean, of course, that everyone fully resolves a loss, or finds a state of "closure". Even the most resilient seem to hold onto at least a bit of wistful sadness. But we are able to keep on living our lives and loving those still present around us.'[1]

Human evolution is a wondrous thing. As evolutionary psychologists like Darwin proposed, and hordes of scientists have since proved, it is the human capacity to adapt to the environment that has enabled us to survive on the planet this long. Evolutionary biologists and psychologists have shown that our bodies are a collection of constantly evolving processes allowing us to hunt, breed, feed, mate and live in a way that increases the odds of survival. Over time—and we're talking thousands of years here—our bodies have adapted to the ways of the world, and they continue to adapt according to changing requirements over centuries and through generations, so that the bodies we inhabit today were formed by the best genetic blueprint evolved from generations of ancestors. In short, we are hard wired for survival; it's in our DNA.

In the second week after the girls died, our sons went back to school, and Trevor and I decided to check with their teachers about how they were doing. We met with the school principal, Simon Leese, keen to glean his insights gathered over decades of school experience as to how children react to losing a sibling. He told us that, while in no way wanting to belittle the enormity of what we were facing, he believed that humans are remarkably able to cope with grief, that we are equipped to handle loss, and that we have an inherent capacity to adapt and survive. Even in the face of such devastating loss. I remember being heartened by his response at the time—it gave us a glimmer of hope. But, 18 months down the track, I am more convinced than ever that what he shared with us that day is a little-said but profound truism of grieving. We might not want to endure the loss, but we have it within us to cope.

WE HAVE AN INHERENT CAPACITY TO ADAPT AND SURVIVE.

Last year I read Wednesday Martin's book *Primates of Park Avenue* after hearing it reviewed on the radio. Martin, a social anthropological researcher who writes for the *New Yorker*, has provided a light-hearted and, at times, scathing account of her experience attempting to assimilate as a new mum in the fiercely competitive world of motherhood on Manhattan's Upper East Side. I now know that the UES (in local parlance) is pretty much *the* pressure-cooker hot spot of parenting on our entire planet: it's hard to find an apartment without having full financial and personality vetting; hard to make new friends without the backing of celebrity connections, a title or a sizeable fortune; impossible to get into kindergarten, let alone schools without long-established local lineage; a perpetual struggle to keep up with the Zeta-Joneses. Much of the book is devoted to her searing descriptions of these highly competitive women who have professionalised motherhood, and her desperate bid to enter their 'tribe' by sporting the right handbag, attending the right parties and helping out at the right charity functions. Towards the end of the book, however, her own miserable experience

CHOOSE HEALING
(WHEN YOU'RE READY, THAT IS)

The Compassionate Friends (TCF) is an American-based network for bereaved parents, each month offering support to over 18,000 people via group meetings and virtual chat rooms. A year after Abi died, I managed to work out the international time differences and log onto one of TCF's online groups. I was curious as to what type of support and chat such a conversation involved.

As a first timer, I was immediately struck by three things: firstly, the number of people participating in this one chat room (a dozen other bereaved parents just like me); second, how utterly terrible it was that three of them were mourning lost sons fighting wars in Iraq and Afghanistan; and, finally, how stuck in their grief they were. I probably shouldn't have been shocked by this, given that their meetings and chat rooms are intended as a place where people can talk, listen, empathise and offer each other emotional support; TCF state very clearly that they don't have professionals running the meetings or giving advice.

I understand that it can be important to express grief and dedicate time to it. I also understand the inappropriateness and futility of rushing through the experience, and the pitfalls of denial, and that these people were (like me) in the first two years of loss. Those present were behaving quite appropriately in expressing their loss and pain, their bitterness and their anger—they were in the right place doing the right thing. But it wasn't the right place for me. Even though I had so much in common with the other bereaved parents, I found the environment too helpless.

The prospect of going over and over events and feelings very quickly filled me with dread. I'm not in any way dismissing the value of chat rooms or support groups (as I describe in Chapter 10, having supportive and empathetic connections is vital during bereavement); it was just that it didn't work for me. As it turned out, this was a good example of me 'being my own experiment' (as I suggested in Chapter 1). I tried it, can fully respect its merit, but I knew instinctively and very quickly that this particular strategy held no benefit for me.

Later that day, reading Sandy Fox's book, *Creating a New Normal . . . After the death of a child*, introduced me to Dr Maurice Turmel. A grief counsellor, speaker and author, Turmel has a very black-and-white approach to grieving that will resonate with some and no doubt appal others. He says: 'There is no substitute for working through your grief if you truly want to heal. Some people simply refuse to move forward, hanging on to their grief as if they were hanging on to their child. They don't accept that they can actually heal and hold on to that precious child in a loving and expansive way rather than continue with their suffering. You have to choose healing in order to recover from grief. You have to commit to your own recovery just like any other person who is stuck in some disabling condition.'[2] Fox and I share the opinion that we have to help ourselves climb out of the abyss and into the sunlight again. Talking it over and over in a chat room proved little help for me. Perhaps if I'd joined months earlier it would have soothed me, but I left the chat room that day feeling more despondent than I had when the hour began. Ultimately, I guess, in the inimitable words of Hamlet, when it comes to action, the readiness is all.

of giving birth to a stillborn baby and the simultaneous tragic death of a friend's three-year-old daughter cause her to reflect on the impact of child mortality on our lives. She does so in a serious tone, and by taking a trained anthropological approach to the subject, brought me back to Simon Leese's words about humans' innate capacity for grief.

As Martin writes, 'We take for granted that our families of two, three, four, five, and even six children will not only survive but also thrive. They will brush off colds and flus and chicken pox, if they get them, bypassing the more awful things—the disfigurers and paralysers and killers such as measles and whooping cough and polio—thanks to immunisations. They will go to school and then to college, our children. They will marry, in time, and have children of their own. They will make us proud. They will bury us. This is our script. And so, as I mothered day to day as one did on the Upper East Side, I didn't contemplate, in any sustained or careful or serious way, just how closely the territories of mothering and loss overlap. It's a secret, until it happens to you.'[3]

Once the unthinkable did happen to her and to her friend, Martin tells of the immense support she received from mothers all around her, prompting her to suggest that 'the software of motherloss' still resides within us, built up over the thousands of years in which infant mortality has been a fact of life. The low infant mortality rate in developed countries today is, after all, a relatively new phenomenon and unique to certain countries. A million babies still die worldwide every day, and 43 per cent of children born into hunter-gatherer communities die before they reach the age of 15.[4]

The long-term impact is that coping with death is as much a part of our fundamental, deep, inherited human experience as finding a mate and having children. It's just that, with the steady medicalisation of healthcare, and our incessant desire to live for longer and our ability to make that happen, we have begun to regard death with outrage, as a failing of the system. A transgression of our fundamental rights and expectations. We have forgotten that death is very much part of the system. The differences in bereavement practices between developed and non-developed countries highlight this fact: in the developed world we've begun to live as though death has no part in our lives. 'In a town like Manhattan, in a tribe as privileged as the one I studied, tragedy hits with a strange double force. You are knocked in the head by the fact of it, first of all, and then by another echoing pain, the knowledge that you are neither cosseted nor safe, in spite of all your attempts to have made it so,' writes Martin.[5]

When she scratched beneath the surface, death was everywhere: 'Just about every mother I knew had lost a child, or her sister or best friend had, in ways that are practically unspeakable. At two weeks pregnant, or at twelve. At thirty-nine weeks, a cord looping its way around the baby's neck . . . The newborn suffocated by the baby nurse who rolls on him in the night in her sleep. The two-year-old who falls at the playground—a little fall, nothing, she didn't even seem to hit her head—and dies of a concussion a few days later. The toddler who tumbles from the window, dying in traffic, breaking every single heart in the city. The one-year-old who goes to the best hospital in town for a simple, straightforward procedure and never comes home. Three girls, swept away in a fire. Here. Right here. In our world. On the Upper East Side, a place that feels safe, a place where anything is possible, until it is not.'[6]

Death doesn't discriminate. Death is everywhere and it happens to us all; all those we love will die or have died. It is both certain and, at times, horrifically random. Knowing this has helped me grieve and process Abi's death. It has prevented me from feeling singled out; diminished the sense of outrage and anger that comes from feeling our family's rights have been violated. Yes, it was waaaaaaaaay too soon. Yes, it's not fair—on Abi, on us, on any of those who loved her. But to deny that people die—even gorgeous twelve-year-old girls who never hurt a fly and have so much to give and do—is to deny the essential truth: that life is tough, chance happens and that people of all ages, stages, religions, places, faces and varying degrees of health die. When people rant and rave and question 'Why me?' in response to the death of someone they love, a small voice inside my head simply answers, 'Why not you, or me, or her?'

COPING WITH DEATH IS AS MUCH A PART OF OUR FUNDAMENTAL, DEEP, INHERITED HUMAN EXPERIENCE AS FINDING A MATE AND HAVING CHILDREN.

During the process of grieving, my thoughts on death have evolved. Now I firmly believe that humans are hard wired to cope. Most of us have it within us to cope, using only very unremarkable processes—the ordinary magic that Masten refers to in her work. Certainly, it is a painful and rarely linear process, and some find it easier than others. I'm the first to acknowledge

I had some advantages that have helped me through this process: being extroverted, optimistic, well supported and sufficiently funded, and having a solution-focused coping style no doubt helped in some way. The research says as much. But, adopting a philosophy that suffering and death are very much part of life acted as a cornerstone of my grief. Why me, why *not* me? Why Abi, why *not* Abi? I understand that death, mistakes and accidents happen, to me and everyone else. Death is universal across the lifespan and across cultures. It helps if we can understand this. Wrapping my head around that took some doing, but it helped.

In the first chapter I referred to long-term studies showing that most people manage to recover from traumatic experiences without any kind of medical or therapeutic intervention. As George Bonanno suggests, 'What is perhaps most intriguing about resilience is not how prevalent is it; rather, it is that we are consistently surprised by it. I have to admit that sometimes even I am amazed by how resilient humans are, and I have been working with loss and trauma survivors for years. As I learned more about how people manage to withstand extremely aversive events, it became all the more apparent to me that humans are wired to survive. Not everybody manages well, but most of us do.'[7]

Accept that you can (and will) adapt to this loss; that although it may require intentional effort on your behalf, it is utterly possible. Above all, you are not alone.

THE FUNDAMENTAL DIFFERENCE BETWEEN OUR *GRIEF REACTIONS* AND *GRIEF RESPONSE*

I came across Thomas Attig's work on bereavement quite late in my grieving. I wish I'd stumbled upon him and his insights earlier, because his work offers a fundamental distinction between two different aspects of grief that were missing pieces from my jigsaw puzzle.

After more than three decades of listening to stories of grief, Attig suggests that bereavement causes a *grief reaction*, by which he means the full range of emotional, psychological, physical, behavioural, social, cognitive and spiritual impacts of bereavement. This reaction is our immediate experience with grief. But, says Attig, there is much more to grief than just grief reaction.

'Many writings on grief stop short with discussions of bereavement and grief reactions, as if stories about them captured the whole of experiences of loss and grief. But . . . grieving is not merely what happens to us as death, bereavement, and grief reactions come into our lives. Grieving is also what we do with what happens to us. Where grief reaction is passive and choiceless, the doing in grieving is active and pervaded with choice. I now prefer to use the term *grieving response* to refer to how we, again as whole persons, actively engage with bereavement and grief reaction emotionally, psychologically, cognitively, behaviourally, socially, and spiritually,' he writes.[8] Accordingly, Attig views the *grieving response* as a process of relearning the world as we adapt and come to terms with our grief reactions and a world transformed by loss.

I find this distinction really helpful. Grief reactions are what happen to us (how we experience loss) and grief responses are how we choose to respond to that loss. 'When we are ready to break away from whatever may be holding us in grief reaction, grieving continues as we actively engage with the realities of what has happened to us and we begin addressing challenges of relearning the world of our experience,' he says, going on to emphasise that the grief response involves active engagement with our grief reactions as much as re-engagement with the world around us.[9]

Grief reactions typically include loneliness, sadness, helplessness, longing, and loss of courage, hope and faith, unsettling questions and intrusive thoughts, homesickness for the familiar, and a range of accompanying physical symptoms. These reactions happen *within us*, just as the loss happens *to us*.

However, grieving is also an active response to both the deprivation of bereavement and the numerous grief reactions we are consumed with. Attig writes, 'We engage with the death and the deprivation and changes in the world of our experience, come to terms with and even learn from our reactions to it, reshape our daily life patterns, and redirect our life stories in the light of what has happened. We respond as the multi-dimensional beings we are: We exert physical energy. We work through and express emotion. We change motivations, habits, and behaviour patterns. We modify relationships. We return home to familiar meanings in life. We reach for inevitably new meanings. And we change ourselves in the process. Death, bereavement, and our grief *reactions* are not matters of choice. But grieving in the quite contrasting second sense of the term as an active *response* to them is pervaded with choice. When ready, we must choose our own path in transforming the course of our lives following bereavement.'[10]

Chapter 6

Secondary losses

IT'S NOT JUST THE LOSS of the loved one that has to be accepted. A raft of what psychologists call 'secondary losses' also require adjusting to. Secondary losses are all the dreams, ambitions, opportunities, future life events and relationships that vanish from your life along with your loved one. The term also relates to the myriad specific roles and functions that person played in your life—the breadwinner, the hairdresser, the novel-finder, the handyman, bridge/golf/tennis partner, chief recycler, meal maker, wood chopper and fire lighter, homework adviser, towel folder, car cleaner, map reader, lunchbox maker, ironer, sober driver, Christmas wrapping expert, dog walker . . . and so the list goes on. Secondary losses may also be financial, or involve the loss of friends, a job, or a home. They can include the loss of the family unit and former stability, loss of faith, and even the loss of confidence in the security and safety of this world (particularly after sudden or violent deaths).

Who are you now that you've lost this important person? Where will all the love you gave them get channelled? What do you do with your future hopes and dreams? What do you need to learn to do, however begrudgingly, now that they are no longer in your life?

In losing Abi, I lost my personal identity and seem to have experienced a personality change. This, apparently, is very common. Where once I was extroverted, upbeat and predominantly happy, I became consumed with sadness and loss. This was all new territory for me. Coming to terms with it required adjustment and acceptance of another secondary loss: I was no longer the person I used to be. I can find myself standing at a party and realise the fun has ebbed away; all I want to do is go home and curl up in bed, the sanctuary of my grief. I'm reminded of the lamentation, 'Happiness has gone out of our lives; grief has taken the place of our dances' (Lamentations 5:15).

'Another loss is the old "you", the person you were before this loss occurred, the person you will never be again. Up till now, you didn't know this kind of sadness. You couldn't even have imagined anything could feel this bad. Now that you are inconsolable, it feels like the new "you" is forever changed, crushed, broken, and irreparable. These temporary feelings will pass, but you will never be restored to that old person. What is left is a new you, a different you, one who will never be the same again or see the world as you once did,' write Elisabeth Kübler-Ross and David Kessler, summing up my feelings adroitly.[1]

Charged with their protection and as promoters of their opportunities, hopes and dreams, our daily interactions with our children in many ways define our sense of self. The day before Abi died I knew, with certainty, who I was and what my life's work entailed. Suddenly all that changed. I remember in the first week following her death saying to one of her favourite school teachers, who was also a family friend, that I no longer knew who I was. 'Last week I was a mother of three, close to finishing my PhD. Now I don't recognise myself,' I told Bridget as we walked on the beach at dusk. 'You'll always be a mother of three,' she replied, and I cried. I will always be a mother of three. Of course I will. She will always be my little girl. Of course she will. But still I needed to be told.

Part of my grieving process has therefore involved me finding ways to honour the fact that we had three children. The easiest is that I intentionally and consistently refer to Paddy as our middle child. It makes me feel good inside every time I say the words. Early on, I'd find myself referring to 'the boys' ('I must go home and check that the boys are eating/getting up/gone to bed/not having a party' and so on), but I modified this to, 'I must go home and check on the kids.' One word changed and Abi was not written out of our lives. Over time I dropped this distinction, but it served me well for a few months by acknowledging her presence in our family.

We've also struggled being a family of four. No offence to families of four, or three, or two, but after twelve years of being a family of five, there was something familiar and complete and 'right' about that odd number. Being a family of four is just too symmetrical, too square, and mainly too small to feel right. I hate being a family of four. It's all wrong. But, over time, we are slowly learning to occupy our new family shape. I distinctly recall taking a photo of the four of us before we headed off tramping last Easter holidays and noticing that I felt okay about the way we were. We look happy in this new family, we were happy in it: just the four of us, learning to be less.

Equally painful was our loss of all things girlie. Not only were we grieving the loss of Abi's specific personality, but also her contribution to our family. As a 12-year-old girl she brought the fun and laughter, the singing and dancing, the giggles and occasional shrill screams. She brought pink and sequins and ballet into our home; she brought friends with bikinis, discarded bracelets, apricot-scented body lotions, fluffy cream dressing gowns, a multitude of ribbons and hairgrips festooned with anything from butterflies to polka dots, an endless desire to bake and decorate cupcakes and to chat over dinner preparations. Planning birthdays and Christmases without her boundless enthusiasm will never be the same.

Since she's gone, we've hankered after her girliness, both in these superficial ways and of course more fundamentally. All of our future hopes and dreams for our dear, beautiful daughter died with her. No walking her down the aisle for Trevor one day; no watching her career with interest and pride (no doubt anxiety and frustration too); no unsuitable boyfriends to fight off or front up to for Ed, Paddy and Trevor; no sitting bikini-clad on strong shoulders at summer festivals; no graduation day, 21sts, bridal shopping trips, or cuddles on Christmas morning. This additional loss hit me hard. I am severed from the Sisterhood. And while I hope there will be girls back with us in due course, in the meantime I profoundly miss their presence in our home and lives.

The loss of my sense of security

The experience of trauma has consequences, chief of which is a heightened sense of physical and emotional vulnerability. On holiday recently, Trevor had a sore throat, which became sufficiently bad to prompt him to get into a taxi and head across an unknown Asian city in search of a late-night doctor. He headed out the door without me giving it a second thought, until, ten minutes later, he sent me pictures of the massive street riot his cab had become embroiled in. Out of nowhere, and out of all proportion to what my brain knew was minimal threat, the familiar anxiety came rushing in. Until I knew he was at the doctor's and had been seen, I felt (very suddenly and acutely) aware of how vulnerable we were. How stupid it was to take anything for granted in this world.

THE EXPERIENCE OF TRAUMA HAS
CONSEQUENCES, CHIEF OF WHICH IS
A HEIGHTENED SENSE OF PHYSICAL
AND EMOTIONAL VULNERABILITY.

Once you've lived with continued aftershocks from earthquakes (which come without warning to shake your world) and received that call from the policeman (saying he's on his way to see you), there is no longer any sense of certainty. Anything is possible, everything is possible, at any time.

How are we supposed to go on living normally, letting our remaining precious children walk out our front door every day, when we have been made so acutely aware of the randomness and fragility of life? Vulnerability is a particularly challenging aspect of bereavement, especially following the loss of a child or anyone deemed 'too young' to die.

Social anthropologist Wednesday Martin sums this up beautifully, when she writes of that 'crazed but logical, urgent-feeling' of the need to hide other children away, to protect them from danger, and the 'obsessive fear that now he or she will be hit by a car or walk into the pool or somehow, anyhow, be extinguished'.[2] But, learning to live with fear and vulnerability is an essential skill of resilience. It's easy to view courage as the absence of fear, but there's plenty of evidence to show (and my experience backs this up) that courage is the ability to experience fear but not become overwhelmed or paralysed by it.

VULNERABILITY IS A PARTICULARLY CHALLENGING ASPECT OF BEREAVEMENT.

I've read a great deal since Abi died, searching for clues to promote acceptance, for contemporary sound bites and ancient wisdoms that add to the jumble of jigsaw pieces that help make sense of my new world. Reading Pema Chödrön first introduced me to two key pieces of the puzzle of life and death. As if they were signposts pointing my energies in the right direction, I very quickly attached myself to the two Buddhist principles of 'Life is Suffering' and what I like to think of as 'The Universal Law of Impermanence'. I'm not a practising Buddhist, but adopting some of Buddhist philosophy has substantially helped me overcome the secondary loss of my trust in the world and my fear of life's random nature. After all, given that Buddha declared, 'I teach suffering, its origin, cessation and path' 2500 years ago, his teachings must be relevant to grieving. Understanding that life is suffering, and that much of that suffering comes from clinging to the illusion of permanence, helps. Approaching life knowing that suffering is a non-negotiable part of it, and that nothing lasts forever, has enabled me to get through the days, focused on the here and now, refusing to worry about what will happen in the future, how long my boys will continue to live healthily for, how long Trevor will stay alive. I am learning to accept that anxieties such as these cause me greater pain and to acknowledge that I have absolutely no control over the impermanence of life. As the Dalai Lama has said: 'The reality of death has always been a major spur to virtuous and intelligent action in all Buddhist societies. It is not considered morbid to contemplate it, but rather liberating from fear.'[3]

Bonanno's longitudinal research following bereaved spouses also reveals the strong relationship between people's views on death and how they cope with bereavement.[4] Having interviewed a probability sample of 1532 married men and women from the Detroit area in 1987–1988 on a wide range of variables, including their world views, social support, family, wellbeing and depression diagnosis (prior to bereavement), Bonanno and his team then followed bereaved participants over three subsequent waves of assessment, evaluating their psychosocial adjustment and resilience specifically over the next five years. Participants' responses to statements like 'Death is simply part of the process of life' and 'I don't see any point in worrying about death' predicted how well they coped with grief. 'People who years earlier said they didn't worry about death or who generally accepted that death happens were the same people who tended to cope best with the pain of grief when their spouse died,' Bonanno explains.[5]

Feeling a heightened sense of vulnerability (worrying about all the things that *might* happen), and having the girly future I had eagerly anticipated wrenched away from me, have been two of the toughest aspects of Abi's death to handle. Understanding that secondary losses are real and warrant my attention has helped. Being aware of them has made me realise how multi-dimensional our loss is and helped me to understand the many different aspects and scope of my grief. Writing about these losses has also helped, forcing me to acknowledge them and consider their impact. And because I like my writings to wrap up in some kind of conclusion, the process encouraged me to make plans regarding ways to cope with them. Secondary losses have a nasty habit of revealing themselves over time, however. Some can be dealt with practically; others are excruciating and have to be endured. They are a work in progress for me.

Exercise in identifying secondary losses

When someone we love dies, we also have to come to terms with other 'secondary losses' that occur as a result of the death (the primary loss).

What secondary losses have you got to cope with? Consider which of the following are secondary losses for you. Financial losses or changes in income? Emotional support? A loss of routine? Have you lost specific friendships? What practical things? Your faith? Are there communities or groups you will no longer see as a result of the primary loss? Have you lost your self-confidence? Your identity? Life purpose or sense of direction? What about your hopes and dreams for the future? Your sense of safety? How have your family roles and duties changed?

Circle the three that most resonate with you, or write your own down. Who can you talk to about these losses? Who recognises the importance of them and will support you? What about putting your thoughts down on paper if you don't want to talk about them, or discussing it in an email with a sympathetic source? Greater awareness brings the opportunity to gradually devise strategies for dealing with these additional losses, and lets others know how and when they can help.

Chapter 7

Positive emotions

BOOKS AND WEBSITES ABOUT grief and mourning feature plenty of information about negative emotions—how important it is to feel them, not repress them, and how fundamental they are to grief. You cannot love and not experience some degree of negative emotions when that loved one dies.

What the traditional bereavement research fails to explain, however, is the transformational power of positive emotions in all stages and aspects of our life, and *especially* while we are grieving. The grief literature might be adept at telling us to accept that experiencing and sharing our negative emotions is key to successful grieving, but it is largely silent on the critical importance of experiencing and sharing positive emotions at this time. This is largely based on ignorance, owing to the fact that academics don't commonly like to consider research findings from beyond their field. So, while plenty of evidence has accrued in psychology over the last three decades detailing the vital importance of positive emotions for our psychological health,[1] most of the researchers publishing in *Death International* (yup, that's the snappy name of the leading bereavement journal) have yet to stumble upon this important and relevant research.

DON'T UNDERESTIMATE THE CRITICAL IMPORTANCE OF EXPERIENCING AND SHARING POSITIVE EMOTIONS AT THIS TIME.

What we do know is that all emotions have been crucial for human survival over the millennia. They are what psychologists call 'adaptive'. That is, emotions have evolved because they help humans respond and adapt in specific ways. For instance, most people are familiar with the fight or flight response which, when invoked by danger or anger, mobilises all our psychological and physiological resources to focus narrowly on the threat, thereby increasing our chances of survival. As this reaction to our emotions increased our chances of survival, so this mechanism has stayed with us through thousands of years of evolution.

While the fight or flight instinct is well known, the adaptive function of positive emotions has until recently been less understood. In 1980, American psychologists Lazarus, Kanner and Folkman suggested that, in the face of adversity, positive emotions may provide psychological time out, as well as sustaining coping efforts and restoring key resources diminished by stress.[2]

Barb Fredrickson, Professor of Psychology at the University of North Carolina, a key researcher in the field of positive emotions, has made it her lifelong academic endeavour to establish the evolutionary purpose of positive emotions. That is, why do we have them; how have they helped humans to adapt and survive through time? She has become well known in psychology for the formulation of her 'Broaden and Build' theory, which posits that positive emotions perform a key adaptive purpose by enabling us to broaden our perspective and discover a greater range of solutions and creativity, and, over time, build our social, intellectual, psychological and even physical resources. In essence, positive emotions do more than just feel good; they actually *do* good.

Fredrickson's research has produced some important findings about positive emotions that are relevant to grieving. For instance, they are fleeting (like any emotional state, feelings of joy, gratitude, interest, awe and contentment typically last only a matter of minutes); they are less intense and less attention-grabbing than negative emotions (which we easily notice); but they also have vitally important downstream outcomes, critical to life and death. These include friendship development, marital satisfaction, higher incomes, better physical health and longevity.[3] A recent review of almost 300 studies concluded that positive emotions are as instrumental in *creating* success and health as they are a reflection of success and health.[4]

Furthermore, Fredrickson has shown the importance of experiencing higher levels of positive emotions for resilience. 'Trying times almost inevitably bring negativity,' she explains. 'Unchecked, the narrowed mindsets of negativity can pull you on a downward spiral and drain the very life out of you. Yet even while unforeseen forces pull you down, you can choose a different course.'[5] Positive emotions can loosen negativity's grip on your mental outlook. Her research shows that positive emotions have remained an essential aspect of human functioning, because they open up our hearts and minds to a broader range of possibilities. When we experience positive emotions, we are more creative solution-makers: we literally see more options available to us, and can therefore access a wider range of solutions. They shift our perspective: 'We can all be astonishingly resilient. Indeed, this is your birthright as a human being. You can bend without breaking. And even when you least suspect it, you can rebound. The good news is that you already have what it takes to bounce back . . . By helping you regain your perspective, moments of joy, love, gratitude, and inspiration remove negativity's blinders and put the brakes on downward spirals. Positivity, I've discovered, is at the heart of human resilience,' Fredrickson continues.

POSITIVE EMOTIONS DO MORE THAN JUST FEEL GOOD; THEY ACTUALLY *DO* GOOD.

In the aftermath of 9/11, when the whole of America was left in post-traumatic shock, Fredrickson says she initially questioned the relevance of her work. What place could positive emotions have in such a world? But then the data from her published studies suggesting positive emotions offer a lifeline in the face of trauma encouraged her to dig deeper into the relationship between positive emotions and resilience. Fredrickson and her team had already measured the resilience levels of more than 100 college students. Now she wondered if they could find the same participants, and measure their levels of positive emotions and resilience in the post-9/11 environment to see whether positive emotions helped them cope through the terrorist attacks and their aftermath. Fredrickson and her colleagues called the students back in and asked them, among other things, to describe the most stressful situation they'd experienced since 9/11 that was in some way related to the attacks, and how often they'd felt a range of positive and negative emotions. They then measured the students' resilience, along with their optimism, tranquillity, life satisfaction and symptoms of depression. Their findings have important implications for anyone living through trauma.

Those students who had reported high resilience scores on the initial pre-9/11 survey did indeed demonstrate greater resilience in the aftermath of the event.[6] They showed the fewest signs of clinical depression. What's more, positive emotions were the secret to their success. Fredrickson and colleagues found a strong association between higher levels of positive emotion and resilient coping styles. 'People who bounced back were not in denial or selfish . . . Mixed in with their suffering and concern, they also experienced positive emotions. These resilient students felt joy, love, and gratitude when connecting with others . . . Perhaps they were inspired and awed by the groundswell of unity and compassion both within their local community and around the globe. Perhaps they were deeply curious about the unfolding world events, and hopeful about the future despite the grim reality of this trying time.'[7] Whatever the source, the experience of positive emotions is what made the difference, effectively applying the handbrake to the students' negative emotions and enabling them to bounce back quickly.

It is true the students participating in this study were not directly involved in the attacks on the Twin Towers and, as far as we know, they weren't grieving. But the fact remains that Fredrickson's studies demonstrate that, even while we experience stress and negative emotions, having positive emotions in our lives, however fleeting and whatever their source, is vital for our resilience. Furthermore, the finding that negativity can sit alongside positivity is also an important discovery for those of us who are grieving.

In the years since Fredrickson published this research, others have reached similar conclusions. Bonanno's work using survey data and intensive interviews from a large representative sample of New York residents (2752 participants) in the six months after the attacks showed that of the 392 participants who had a friend or relative killed on 9/11, 54 per cent were assessed as resilient.[8] Similarly, positive emotions have been shown to interrupt and reduce the influence of negative emotions among grieving widows;[9] it has also been shown that a significant proportion of older adults manage to experience positive emotions during bereavement. A more recent study by Ong, Bergeman and Boker, which investigated diary data from 300 older adults aged between 60 and 90 years, reached the same conclusion: compared to participants low in resilience, highly resilient individuals reported greater engagement in, and responsiveness to, daily positive events.[10]

As is the way in scientific research, once we've established a connection exists, further studies examine the reasons for these associations. In an online grief column for *Positive Psychology News Daily*, friend and colleague Kathryn Britton discusses the potential mechanisms at work by exploring the connections between experiencing positive emotions and maintaining important relationships during bereavement. She writes, 'Bonanno describes mourning as an oscillation between sadness and other emotions, often positive ones including love, humour, curiosity, and awe. That's my experience. I think of the sadness of grief as waves that rise, crest, and then roll away, sometimes at surprising times and with huge intensity. But in between, I have done a lot of laughing, telling stories, and remembering the quirky marvellous things about the person that is gone.'[11] Britton has had six people die in her immediate circle in the last five years.

She continues by describing her own theory on why positive emotions are important for grief: 'We laugh at stories about goofy things our loved ones did, we remember them with love, we discuss their positive qualities with awe, we have new experiences with other mourners that bring positive emotions. People used to think that positive emotions in the face of grief were a sign of denial (one of those Kübler-Ross stages). In their bereavement research, Bonanno and Keltner found that the more people laughed and smiled during the months after losing a spouse, the better their mental health evaluations over two years of bereavement.

'Perhaps it's like coming up for air. Perhaps, also, it lightens the atmosphere around them making it easier for other people to stay by them. So perhaps positive emotions help keep their social connections with others going. As a friend of a bereaved spouse and bereaved parents, I certainly want them to have all the sad time they need. But I also find it a relief when we can laugh together.

'So instead of five solid stages, think of grief as an oscillation between sadness and other emotions, often positive. The oscillation can occur frequently over the course of a day. The sadness lets us adjust to the loss. The other emotions allow us to engage with the world around us.'

Healthy grieving involves a wide range of emotions. I am certainly not suggesting that all anger, sadness, guilt and anxiety must be minimised during bereavement—that makes no sense at all. A resilient person experiences all emotions; they just don't get stuck in one particular emotion. As Harvard psychologist Tal Ben-Shahar says, 'The first thing to do to become happier, paradoxically, is to accept painful emotions, to accept them as a part and parcel of being alive. You know, there are two kinds of people who don't experience painful emotions such as anxiety or disappointment, sadness, envy; two kinds of people who don't experience these painful emotions. They are the psychopaths and the dead. So if we experience painful emotions at times, it's actually a good sign. It means that we're not a psychopath and we're alive. And the paradox is that when we give ourselves the permission to be human, the permission to experience the full gamut of human emotion, we open ourselves up to positive emotions as well.'[12]

A RESILIENT PERSON EXPERIENCES ALL EMOTIONS; THEY JUST DON'T GET STUCK IN ONE PARTICULAR EMOTION.

Full emotional expression is an essential part of being resilient. That doesn't mean being falsely positive but rather finding the people, places and activities that prompt the experience of positive emotions. We know that negative emotions abound in grief; we're looking to balance them out with some of the positive emotions too. Ultimately, as my friend Dr Elaine O'Brien counsels: 'I found that it was easier and more comforting to think of "appropriate emotions" during grief. I had a friend who would often, and innocently, ask me, "What's good?" I didn't/don't mean to be a downer, but sometimes this put me over the edge. When things seemed overwhelming, it was hard to put on a good front, a good face. I felt more honest and true embracing my raw sadness and distress at times. It didn't feel right, and it actually felt bad to force happy feelings. It felt more true to accept the presence of emotions without judging them.'[13]

In his book, Bonanno describes how part of the evolutionary purpose of emotions is that we show them to others—sparking the necessary response from those around us. 'We have . . . literally hundreds of individual muscle actions. For evolution to have resulted in such an elaborate system, the facial display of emotion must have carried great survival value,' he explains.[14] For example, a look of disgust warns others to stay away (thereby keeping them from poisonous foods or damaging gases). So, what is the likely value of sadness? According to evolutionary psychologists, sadness facilitates adjustment to the loss: by focusing our attention inwards, and enabling us to take stock and readjust, it promotes deeper and more effective reflection. Essentially, sadness enforces time out, so that the evolutionary benefit of sadness is to prompt others to care for us. Deep and sustained introspection, accompanied by tears, clearly signals to others that we are in need of their help to survive. Isn't human adaptation clever? Other bereavement researchers suggest just a small increase in positive emotions has beneficial effects.[15]

To consider this from a practical perspective, it helps to start by listing *all* the positive emotions available to us. This draws our attention to their broad range. Experiencing positive emotions doesn't merely equate to being happy, but instead includes being curious, humorous and loving; feeling pride, awe, hope, inspiration and gratitude, and the quieter emotions such as serenity.

Outlined below are some of the positive emotions I have found helpful during my grieving. Consider how each emotion may support you as you journey through grief. Which positive emotions do you experience frequently; which could you do with intentionally seeking out and topping up on?

Curiosity

It took a while for my curiosity to kick in after the girls died, but somewhere in the second year I started reading. And reading and reading. I devoured anything I could get my hands on to describe and explain what I was going through; how and why I was feeling this maelstrom of emotions, tiredness and forgetfulness. I read academic journals, self-help books, personal accounts, poetry anthologies, one whole book dedicated to eulogies, blogs, psychology department websites, dissertations, newspaper and magazine articles.

> CURIOSITY PUT MY OWN BEREAVEMENT
> EXPERIENCE INTO PERSPECTIVE AND
> WAS THEREFORE REASSURING.

I was looking for answers, I guess. I wanted to know the truth of what was happening to me, and (of course) how long it might last. But what I very rapidly sensed was that this curiosity was helpful. There were benefits in trying to understand what was going on inside my head and my body; it stopped me from thinking I was going mad; it soothed me to read other people's experiences, to find so many similarities between their journey and my own. I became aware that, far from being alone, I was walking a well-trodden path navigated by many others before me, and that everything I was feeling and doing was normal. Curiosity put my own bereavement experience into perspective and was therefore reassuring.

What are you curious about?
What would you like to find out more about?

Pride

Over these past terrible months, I have at times experienced such immense pride it literally felt as if my heart would burst. I know it sounds naff, but when I look around and see what people are doing for us, how all of us are soldiering on in spite of the girls' deaths, I get a sensation of physical expansion around my solar plexus that almost hurts. Pride at our sons, for all that they have achieved despite the odds, at how they've carried themselves and gone on to live good and full lives without their little sister; pride at my wider family for their empathy and immense capacity for love, compassion and thoughtfulness; pride at our local community for all the practical and emotional support they've given us, instinctively and in abundance—with no timelines attached. Pride has helped me notice the others in my life and strengthened those bonds. Seeing the boys and Trevor carry on encourages me to carry on too.

What in your life makes you proud?
If you stop to think about it, who has made you proud these past months?
What about yourself? What have you achieved or overcome that you can be proud of?

Awe

In September 2014 we were lucky enough to get away for a week to the Australian coast. One day, walking up to the lighthouse in beautiful Byron Bay, Trevor and I saw a pod of whales diving and leaping way out at sea. We stood, transfixed for a moment, staring at them and imagining life as a whale—at least, I was. As we stood there, side by side, not able to draw our eyes away from them, hungry for one more opportunity to see them dive and soar upwards, breaking the ocean's surface, we discussed how such awe-inspiring experiences may impact our resilience. If positive emotions broaden and build us, I asked, how does that work when we experience awe? Watching whales in their natural habitat makes us feel small, he replied. Their massive size and huge strength, their unknown world, makes our own world seem tiny and insignificant in comparison. Awe broadens our perspective.

He was right. Seeing these magnificent mammals reminded me that I'm part of a bigger universe, a tiny part of something bigger than just us and our life problems. A similar thing had happened when, a few months after the girls died, I had a desperate urge to go walking in the mountains, up to see the Rob Roy Glacier in Mount Aspiring National Park. My friend Marion and I skittered over frozen paths and clambered over rocks until we reached the top, stared at the glacier and the ancient mountains around us, and wept. Life is huge, we said, enormous, unfathomable and vast. Being up there, though, somehow felt better.

When was the last time you felt awe?
Where could you go to that would fill you with awe?

Hope

Writing about hope makes my chest tighten. Hope is the fuel that fires us to move forward in the world. The word for the alternative—hopelessness—says it all. I experienced hopelessness for the first time after Abi died; I woke up one morning in that first week and was shocked to find myself thinking, 'I hate my life.' For someone who has always felt appreciation for all the good things, this was probably my bleakest moment.

HOPE STRENGTHENS MY RESOLVE AND DETERMINATION TO FORGE FORWARD.

I'm not sure what drives my hope, but I do know I'm not giving up on it. When I look back at the blogs I wrote in that first year, flickers of hope are apparent. I hope, for example, that our sons will 'one day marry wonderful, caring women willing to share their hearts'. More recently I've been given a new form of hope. Working my way through the new bereavement science, reading stories of loss from websites like Tom Attig's, has sparked kernels of hope that we will manage to get through this awful process.[16] That, while we will never stop loving or missing Abi, we will over the years learn to live with her loss, and go on to live full and meaningful lives. Having hope strengthens my resolve and determination to forge forward and hate my life much less than I did that day in June 2014.

Given that the worst thing has happened, what are you
hoping for now?

Inspiration

Inspiration keeps me going. Tales of others who have endured terrible life stories inspires me to get up and keep going. Day in day out. Charney and Southwick have found, across multiple interviews, that having a role model, or even role models, is a key factor promoting resilience. 'Role models can be found in one's own life (like your parents) or even people you don't know who are inspirational and have been through something similar. We heard a lot about this from the prisoners of war, who when they were in prison took the other prisoners as role models—many of whom were offered early release but said none of us will go until we all are released together.'[17]

In the course of researching this book, I've stumbled upon many inspirational role models who have given me the strength to keep going. One of them is Carolyn Moor, founder of the Modern Widows Club (www.modernwidowsclub.com). Following the sudden death of her husband on Valentine's Day in 2000, after their vehicle was struck by a car as they returned from dinner, Moor established the MWC, a community of widows aimed at empowering each other to 'lean into life, build resilience and release their potential to make a positive difference in the world'. From just three widows meeting in Moor's home in Florida in 2011, MWC grew to include 3000 members and over 12,000 followers on Facebook by 2015. Inspiration motivates us to keep on pushing forward, to keep trying, as we notice how others have endured tremendous loss and still managed to survive.

Who inspires you?
What stories have you heard that have helped you?

Gratitude

Gratitude helps us deal with our grief by enabling us to focus on what we have, rather than exclusively focusing on what we have lost. Even without Abi here, I am grateful for many things. Firstly, for the family I have left—for Trevor, Ed and Paddy, and all the purpose and reason they bring to my life, but also for the love they give me. I'm grateful for the opportunity to continue to live when Sally, my dear friend, wasn't given that chance. She embodied beauty, spontaneity and generosity, and I'm determined to carry on that legacy. I'm grateful every morning I wake up to see Trevor is still alive, to have him by my side for another day. I am grateful for my amazing family and friends, for *everything* they did for us in those first few days, weeks and months. I'm grateful for their patience and willingness to embark on this long, long journey with us, and never complain at the pace of our recovery, for never expecting us to 'get over' Abi's loss or stop thinking about her.

> GRATITUDE HELPS BY ENABLING
> US TO FOCUS ON WHAT WE HAVE,
> RATHER THAN EXCLUSIVELY FOCUSING
> ON WHAT WE HAVE LOST.

It's easy to see how gratitude helps me take a broader look at my life, to consider the boys as much as I consider Abi. My gratitude at having the chance to live when Sally is dead spurs me on when I'm feeling flat and lacklustre and don't really want to do anything. How can I not walk out to Boulder Bay, join friends for a drink, or prepare a family meal when she no longer has any of these opportunities? What kind of a friend does that make me? Occasionally I put three stones in my pocket—good old Kiwi river stones—as a physical reminder of the things I am grateful for that day. Gratitude forces me to look beyond what I've lost.

What are you grateful for?
Who are you grateful for?

Serenity

In the days after the girls died, it wasn't easy to find peace. Living with a maelstrom in my head, a house full of people, colliding thoughts and emotions, and so many decisions to make, serenity was elusive. And yet. By retiring to bed, shutting myself away in our room, picking up a book, putting on headphones, driving someone home, I did find some quiet moments. Even amid all the chaos, my brain's fundamental desire for serenity expressed itself by repeating words of an old favourite hymn: 'Speak through the earthquake, wind and fire . . . o still, small voice of calm, o still, small voice of calm'. Those words kept urging me to find some stillness and calm amid the madness.

Where can you find some calm?
What do you have to do to secure five minutes alone for yourself?

Humour

Trevor uses humour all the time, and I'm glad to say there's plenty of it. I have never felt bad about laughing, even in those first few hours after we were told of Abi's death. Sitting in the back of the police car, as we were driven five hours to the hospital to identify our daughter, Trevor, Ed, Paddy and I shared stories of our beautiful girl—how much she'd made us laugh, how ridiculous and infuriating she could be. Whoever said never speak ill of the dead? We have laughed and laughed about how annoying she was, pushing her food around her plate, pathetically attempting to brush the massive knots from her hair, how easily baited by the boys she was, how she'd scrunch up her face in fury. Her mad dances, made up on the spot, but allegedly forged from hours of practice.

It's easy to see how laughter bonds us to others in the face of grief; it cements our memories and brings us closer. There's now even good evidence explaining why we sometimes find ourselves laughing at inappropriate times—laughing in the face of death. Proper, cackling laughter (Duchenne laughter, as psychologists refer to it) has been shown to be significantly associated with reduced anger and increased enjoyment among bereaved spouses, as well as with increased enjoyment, better social relationships and disassociation from distress. People who genuinely laughed and smiled more when talking about their loss coped better over the first two years of their bereavement than those who did not.[18]

A few months after the girls died, I was invited to go to a local school's LipSynch night. Knowing that the on-stage entertainment meant I wouldn't have to spend the evening talking to the entire community, but could just watch the acts, I went along. I also went because I knew that it was always a fun night out, and having a bloody good laugh would help, providing some respite from the frequency and intensity of negative emotion, and topping up my quota of positive emotions.

Which of your friends can still make you laugh?
Which films, podcasts or TV shows can you turn to for an easy laugh?

Love

There's always been love during the pain of our bereavement. Bereavement is about love, after all—the love you had for another person. The love you have for them still. The great thing about love, of course—its evolutionary purpose—is that it connects us to others. Feeling love prompts us to reach out, to include others, to look beyond ourselves. Love broadens us and builds our social resources. When the worst happens, it is our social networks and resources that we rely on. In the face of Abi's death, I have vowed to love more.

Exercise in finding positive emotions

Because positive emotions are fleeting and often go unnoticed— unlike negative emotions which tend to hang around—there's much to be gained by actively seeking them out. Don't get me wrong: I'm not suggesting that while you are experiencing a prolonged bout of depression you beat yourself up about not wanting to attend a comedy club. What I am suggesting is that you try to recognise these emotions as they occur in your life, and notice the opportunities to experience more of them.

I have come to think of experiencing positive emotions as investing (i.e. paying deposits) into my psychological piggy bank—which, let's face it, I am now raiding regularly, with daily, at times hourly, bouts of sadness and worry. Knowing my resources are being constantly depleted helps me to focus on re-investing in them via sleep and positive emotions. It reminds me to give space and opportunity for positive emotions to arise: to find the time to explore things that make me curious, embrace humour and feel the cathartic nature of laughter, to use moments of serenity to take stock and feel gratitude for the good things; to look up at the sky, the weather, the moon, and down at the caterpillar and daises with awe. All these emotions were given to us for a reason. Value and feel them all.

Taking a look at the full complement of positive emotions listed below and spend a moment considering where and how you can find these in your own life:

	Where?	*When?*
Curiosity:		
Pride:		
Awe:		
Hope:		
Inspiration:		
Gratitude:		
Serenity:		
Humour:		
Love:		

TWO STRATEGIES FOR PROMOTING POSITIVE EMOTIONS

1 Savour the past, present and future

Fred Bryant is the leading social scientist investigating *savouring*— that is, thoughts or behaviours capable of generating, intensifying and prolonging enjoyment. According to Bryant, 'being able to handle negative events in ways that reduce distress does not guarantee one will experience positive events in ways that promote well-being'.[19] In other words, being good at coping is not enough to make us happy; happiness requires that we are able to appreciate life's good moments.

Savouring helps us get more bang for our buck from positive experiences, partly because it can be carried out across three different time frames: we can reminisce about an event (a holiday with our loved one, a funny moment we shared); we can work hard to be more mindful and use all five senses to enjoy good experiences as they occur; and we can anticipate the future (fantasise or dream about upcoming events). Bryant's research shows savouring is an effective way of building positive emotions, promoting optimism, and that people who savour are more confident and gratified, less hopeless and neurotic.

2 #HTGS

I follow Karen Reivich on Instagram and often see her posting about moments she's grateful for. I recall her teaching us about the negativity bias (how humans are hard wired to notice the bad things that happen more readily than the good), and love her #htgs posts designed to override that negativity bias by encouraging us to 'hunt the good stuff'. HTGS is a technique Reivich and colleagues use to promote positive emotions, gratitude and optimism in the Comprehensive Soldier and Family Fitness programme they've been running with the US Army. It evolved from an exercise in which American psychologists Martin Seligman, Tracy Steen, Nansook Park and Christopher Peterson asked participants to focus on three good things that occurred in their day, and the role they played in those good things. The results of this study were astounding, showing that those people assigned to the three good things condition reported greater levels of happiness and decreased symptoms of depression for up to six months afterward. Cultivating a habit of noticing the good things in life helps increase your quota of daily positive emotions.

Chapter 8

Distraction

IN THE FIRST YEAR after Abi's death, my near-constant thoughts of her almost drove me mad. My immediate thoughts on waking would be of her—nothing concrete, nothing in particular, just a profound knowledge that she's not here anymore, that she's gone forever, and a deadness, a longing gnawed deep inside. I used to play games in my head, resolving that, instead of thinking constantly of Abi, I'd redirect my attention to thoughts about my (incredible and living) boys. What are *they* up to right now? What are *their* favourite clothes, what are *their* opinions of this or that? What do *they* look like? How do *they* smell? Essentially, I would attempt to transfer the type of questions that would circle round and round in my head about Abi to them—just to give myself a break from the constant obsession with her, which was exhausting, not natural and made me feel quite bonkers. Less than a minute into this exercise I'd call it off, accepting the futility. Frustratingly, I simply could not dwell on them and the minutiae of their lives in the way I kept thinking about her.

This habit of dwelling on negative thoughts, chewing them over and over in our minds, is referred to by psychologists as 'rumination'. When rumination is short-lived it can be useful, helping us to organise our thoughts, work out what went wrong and how we can avoid similar situations in future. But, when we ruminate over long stretches of time, covering the same ground over and over again, rumination is not beneficial. Chronic rumination can amplify our negative mood, exacerbating the pain, and rarely leads to effective solutions.

In the face of such endless rumination, I therefore had to find other things to consume my attention. Work helped. Being with other people and talking about other things helped. When my thoughts of Abi, and the constant longing, became too oppressive, I'd contact a friend or colleague and ask to meet, to walk the dog, catch up for a ten-minute coffee break, make a Skype call to discuss some aspect of work that required my total concentration. Anything to pull me out of the introspection and allow my brain some time off.

Accordingly, I was pleased to read an academic paper suggesting that 'coping is embedded in everyday life experience, which involves taking time off from grieving, as when watching an engrossing TV programme, reading, talking with friends about some other topic, or sleeping'.[1] The researchers, Margaret Stroebe and Henk Schut, regard grieving as a dual process as we oscillate backwards and forwards, at times confronting and at others avoiding our grief in order to get some respite. The dual process refers both to this oscillation between confrontation and avoidance, and to the fact that the bereaved have to cope with two types of stressors: *loss-oriented stressors* and *restoration-oriented stressors*. In other words, we have to deal with the loss experience itself (thinking about the dead person, remembering life as it was, looking at old photos, going over the circumstances and events surrounding the death, crying about the loss) and the stress of working out how we are going to live without the deceased in the future (dealing with finances and loneliness, perhaps moving home, learning to cook, paying the bills, and so on).

WE OSCILLATE BACKWARDS AND
FORWARDS, AT TIMES CONFRONTING
AND AT OTHERS AVOIDING OUR GRIEF
IN ORDER TO GET SOME RESPITE.

In stark contrast to Kübler-Ross's model, Stroebe and Schut do not believe in phases of bereavement. 'We do not propose a sequence of stages, but rather a waxing and waning, an ongoing flexibility, over time. Early in bereavement, loss orientation dominates, later on attention turns more and more to other sources of upheaval and distress. At times the bereaved will be confronted by their loss, at other times they will avoid memories, be distracted, or seek relief by concentration on other things.'[2]

This dual process seems to resonate with the bereaved I've interviewed. Claire Rushton, who lost her 16-year-old daughter Courtenay to meningitis in 2014, describes this process as 'dipping my toe into the water', the water representing life outside of her grief. 'By slicing up each experience, a social engagement, or simply a trip to the shops or supermarket which were and still can be completely overwhelming, the hurdles are smaller and my emotions aren't swamped. It's like testing the waters to see what I can handle. Some days I can get my whole foot in, other days it's just too much,' she explains, describing the process of approach and withdrawal at different times of her grief.[3] Stroebe and Schut stress that oscillation is necessary for optimal mental and physical health adjustment. 'The person may choose to take "time off", be distracted, or need to attend to new things, or at times it may be too painful to confront some aspect, leading to voluntary suppression.'[4]

Camille Wortman, another academic focused on grief and bereavement, explains that finding engaging activities to distract us from thoughts is an effective strategy used for combatting depression. 'It is certainly clear from the research evidence, as well as from my personal experience, that distraction can be an important element in the mourning process. Yet almost nobody talks about it,' she wrote to me.[5]

WE CAN USE SMALL ACTIVITIES AS A BRIDGE TO HELP US RETURN TO THE WORLD OF THE LIVING.

'Being involved in an engaging activity can break the grip of negative thoughts, at least temporarily. Examples of engaging activities include going shopping, attending a sporting event with a friend, taking your dog for a walk, or going to the library. Involvement in an engaging activity will increase positive affect (that is positive emotion) more than involvement in an activity that is less engaging. However, experts concur that involvement in just about any activity is better than not being involved. Because bereavement is often accompanied by a profound loss of interest in life, it may be difficult for mourners to become engaged in particular tasks. A strategy for breaking through mourners' resistance is to encourage them to spend five minutes on a potentially engaging task, and telling them that they can stop after that. In most cases, mourners continue with the task once they are drawn into it.'[6]

Claire Rushton has found this is a strategy that works for her. 'There are days that I just can't move and I don't want to, I just want to sit and be sad and for the world to stop.' But she's found her own way of drawing herself back. 'It may sound odd but I tell myself . . . okay, you've cried now, now you need to get up and do something. I call it the "cleaning out the teaspoon drawer moment". I have come to realise that by giving myself permission to be sad and grieve, but also giving myself a reason to take me out of that grief, even if that's all I'm doing—cleaning the crumbs from the teaspoon drawer—I've moved, and the movement switches my emotions from despondency to a purpose again.' Rushton's teaspoon drawer is a good metaphor for the small activities we use as a bridge to help us return to the world of the living.

I sometimes use a similar strategy to approach work. When I'm feeling tired and overwhelmed I find a really easy, mundane task to get started on, knowing that the rest will follow once I've overcome the initial inertia. Work in itself has provided me with the perfect distraction. Before I learned about oscillation from Stroebe and Schut, I had worried that perhaps I was using work as a form of denial. But now I recognise its value as respite: I wasn't hiding from grief, just recovering. Believe me, there was plenty of grieving going on before, after and sometimes even during work hours.

In direct contrast to old-school bereavement theories, these researchers are adamant that this form of denial is in fact a beneficial strategy for the bereaved to adopt—as long as denial is not extreme and/or persistent. 'Confrontation with the reality of loss is the essence of adaptive grieving. It needs to be done, the cognitive business needs to be undertaken, but not relentlessly, and not at the expense of attending to other tasks that are concomitant with loss. It needs "dosage".'[7] Dosage refers to the different levels of grief individual people can bear before requiring a rest from their grieving—using Claire Rushton's terminology, how far we can dip our toe into the water before we need to withdraw. We can't grieve all the time, but we also can't avoid it entirely—there are aspects of the death we are forced to face eventually. Neither confrontation nor avoidance is sustainable, and both the processes of actively grieving and respite from grieving are vital for recovery.

Across the months I've been aware of oscillating not only between positive emotions and negative emotions, and approach and withdrawal, but also backwards and forwards in terms of functioning progress. One week I feel I am coping really well, feeling bright and cheerful and full of purpose, and then, without much warning, I'm weeping and desolate. Yesterday, for example, I cried about eight times, though the week before I'd been feeling really good. Having grieved over my mother, I'm at least aware that this is very common in bereavement. The gaps between bad patches seem to get longer and longer—at first there's only a good day, then I'll have a good few days, a week, or even a few weeks—and then, suddenly, I start to feel blue, a bit lacklustre, and the world turns flat again. Forward and back, forward and back the gradual progress goes.

Conjuring a mental picture of how we oscillate (approaching and withdrawing, approaching and withdrawing, up and down, back and forth) has helped me through the days and weeks. Sometimes there's just no avoiding all those emotions, and I find the strength to lean into them, experience the lot and, in doing so, seem to get out the other side. At others I know I need to withdraw and avoid confronting my grief, even if momentarily.

Distracting activities give us the opportunity to recover, to build up our strengths, so we can do it all again. Similarly there are times when we need to retreat: to lick our wounds, put our heads on the table, and lie down exhausted. Approach, retreat, approach, retreat. And so it goes.

Here's a list of the things I use to snap me out of my grief when it's too debilitating and I know I need a break:

- Music—Spotify is my saviour, offering something for every mood. Don't underestimate the power of music either to shift your mood when you get down or, at other times, just to reflect your feelings.

- Listen to podcasts—'Desert Island Discs' is my favourite because it takes people of wildly different backgrounds through their life stories and reminds me that most people experience massively unpredictable twists and turns and yet still get somewhere in the end.[8]

- Phone a friend—someone I know will make me laugh (usually my sister).

- Walk the dog—mad Jack, the Jack Russell terrier, always makes for a good diversion as he chases the shadows of seagulls or any passing motorbikes.

- Read—my Kindle is my number one source of distraction, particularly in the middle of the night when my mind is not a place I want to linger in.

- Netflix—spending time with my '*other* favourite men' (that's you, Ragnar Lothbrok, Tommy Shelby or even those idiots from *Top Gear*) works without fail.

- Going to the movies with Trevor (my real-life favourite man).

- Cooking/baking.

- Meeting friends for a drink.

Exercise in finding distractions

Distraction is important because grieving is an exhausting business. Do whatever occupies your thoughts and consumes your attention. Don't be hard on yourself: if that means watching entire TV series, or getting lost in movies, or listening to talking books, then do it.

On the next page, list five things you can do to help take your mind off your loss. Remember, they don't all have to be worthy. Claire Rushton's tidying the teaspoon drawer is a great example of a simple activity she finds achievable and sufficiently distracting to draw her out of her grief and back into the world.

Five ways to distract your thoughts

1. _____

2. _____

3. _____

4. _____

5. _____

When you are lying on the couch, or stuck in bed, which one of these is simple and accessible enough to get you up?

Chapter 9

Three habits of resilient thinking

PSYCHOLOGISTS HAVE BEEN INVESTIGATING the impact of our thinking processes on our resilience for more than three decades. Back in the classrooms at UPenn, Karen Reivich went to great lengths to explain that the way we think has a substantial impact on the way we feel and function. 'Research conducted around the world shows conclusively that how we analyse the events that befall us has a profound effect on our resilience. How you respond to situations reflects something called thinking style. Thinking style is like a lens through which we view the world. Everyone has such a lens, and it colours the way we interpret the events of our life. Your thinking style determines your level of resilience—your ability to overcome, steer through, and bounce back when adversity strikes,' Reivich and Andrew Shatté explain in their book, *The Resilience Factor*.[1]

Realistic optimism

Recent psychological studies have demonstrated that optimism is a key protective mechanism against depressive symptoms in the face of trauma, regardless of individuals' culture of origin.[2]

Back in March, nine months after the girls died, I wrote a piece on my blog (www.1wildandpreciouslife.com) about trusting the process.[3] Looking at it now, I can detect the optimism I felt. Not a full-blown clarion cry of optimism—I was still far too bruised for that—but a certain faith that somehow we'd get through. 'As I try to wrap my head around what has happened to our family, and step uncertainly towards our own unknown future, I find myself resurrecting the mantra of one of my university professors, who, when navigating new terrain, constantly reminded us to "Trust the Process",' I wrote, going on to explain that 'trusting the process doesn't imply inertia, rather embarking on small steps forward in the belief that they'll get you there in the end'.

At the time, I wouldn't have recognised this as optimistic thinking. But, reviewing old lecture notes in which Reivich taught that 'being conscious that the present might be bad but to keep looking forward to the future' is the very essence of optimism practised by resilient people, I can see how my attitude fits this mould. She also told us that optimists focus on solutions when change is possible, and use acceptance and humour when it's not. They're also more accurate in their assessment of how much control they have, and less likely to deny and avoid problems.

I would not have described myself as optimistic through the first year after losing Abi but, in psychological terms, I can now see that I was. I turned away from being identified as a 'victim', baulking at the helpless connotations of that phrase; I knew what I could change and what I couldn't. I knew there was no bringing Abi back, but I hoped we could find a way to get through the loss and survive it with our marriage, family and sanity intact.

OPTIMISTS FOCUS ON SOLUTIONS WHEN CHANGE IS POSSIBLE, AND USE ACCEPTANCE AND HUMOUR WHEN IT'S NOT.

Reivich and Shatté explain how this kind of flexible thinking style relates to resilience. 'The most resilient people are those who have cognitive flexibility and can identify all the significant causes of the adversities they face . . . They are realists in that they don't ignore the factors that are permanent or pervasive. Nor do they waste their valuable reserves of resilience ruminating about events or circumstances outside of their control. They channel their problem-solving resources into the factors they can control, and, through incremental change, they begin to overcome, steer through, bounce back and reach out.'[4]

The key words for me here are flexible and realist. In the lecture theatre, Reivich drummed it into us, time and again, that 'realistic optimism' is the key. On the basis that studies have demonstrated the pitfalls associated with runaway optimism (or as she would call it 'Pollyanna optimism', whereby people always assume everything will turn out for the best), realistic optimism requires maintaining a positive outlook without denying reality, appreciating the positive aspects of any given situation without overlooking the negatives. Resilience requires an accurate appraisal of the situation—extreme pessimism and extreme optimism only end in (more) tears.

To sum up, people who can think realistically and optimistically seem to work better with what they've got, differentiating more effectively between things they can change and things that are set, and working out a viable plan to deal with the elements that *are* in their control.

Redefining hope: What are you hoping for now?

The Chronicles of Narnia were my favourite books when I was a child. I remember how much I cried, at 13, when Aslan died. Decades later I went to see *Shadowlands*, the movie, with Trevor and my mum. In it, Anthony Hopkins, playing C.S. Lewis, the author of the Narnia books, describes his grief at his wife's diagnosis with cancer and her death. The three of us sat in the cinema and sobbed. Years later, I still remember the words: 'the pain now is part of the happiness then'.

Flicking through his memoir *A Grief Observed* more recently, I was struck by C.S. Lewis's description of the happiness he and his wife, Joy, found together even 'after all hope was gone'.[5] It struck a chord with me and sent me scuttling off to re-read old lecture notes from one of my professors who described the power of hope in the context of death and grief. Chris Feudtner is one of those professors a student never forgets. A pediatrician at CHOP, the Children's Hospital of Philadelphia, Feudtner told us how he uses psychological hope theory in his work in the children's oncology department. I remember wondering what hope could possibly be present in such a place. Then he relayed to us Mason's story.

Mason was three months old, and had already been in the hospital for two months when Feudtner met him and his family. Mason had a metabolic disease, and his parents had been told a week earlier that it was terminal. Feudtner recalled the moment when he asked the parents, 'Given what Mason is up against, what are you hoping for?' This, at first glance, seems like an absurdly insensitive question. What were they hoping for? For Mason to live, obviously, but they'd just been told that wasn't going to happen. As far as they were concerned, all hope was gone.

But the rest of the story that Feudtner relayed that day gave us, his students, a remarkable and unique insight into the power and nature of hope. Until Feudtner became involved in Mason's case, the hospital team's goal was to get the baby to put on weight. But after careful coaxing and patient discussion with the parents, this remarkable doctor managed to discover that their greatest remaining hopes for Mason were to stop further testing, take him home, have him baptised, and for him to live what time he had left at home among his family. So that's what they did. Mason went home with his family that day; he was baptised and died peacefully three weeks later. A year later, Mason's parents went on to have twins.

Chris Feudtner described how inquiring about new hopes palpably changed the mood in the room for those parents, and the course of Mason's treatment. 'We had confirmed the worst news for parents but left them with hopes to look forward to. Pediatric palliative care is not all sad, there are moments of joy and celebration as to what it means to be alive,' he explained.

This experience had a huge impact on his career, which now sees him work with patients and their families around the notion of hope, even in the direst circumstances. 'There are so many parents who feel lost because once the big hope was shut down nobody thinks to nurture their other hopes. In the face of no curative options, parents need a new goal to strive for.' He now works to ensure that parents at CHOP get the chance to collaborate in the decision-making around their children's outcomes by asking them quite simply, 'So, what are you hoping for now?' Answers to this question demonstrate that hope isn't a single entity—humans don't have just one hope, but a collection of smaller hopes. In the face of even terrible news, of something as final as death, other hopes remain or emerge; the process of hoping endures. Identifying these hopes is important.

HOPE ISN'T A SINGLE ENTITY—HUMANS DON'T HAVE JUST ONE HOPE, BUT A COLLECTION OF SMALLER HOPES.

In the immediate aftermath of the girls' deaths my focus quickly became about reducing additional stress and narrowing my priorities and expectations. Setting myself a new goal of surviving, which started with just aiming for 'mainly functioning', I narrowed the goal posts to accept that any day I got out of bed and went through the motions of vaguely functioning was an achievement. My goals had shifted overnight and, while it was easy to think that all hope had gone, I still had other life goals and priorities.

Knowing what it was that I was aiming for (having a goal, however small) helped me work out which actions to take and changed my definition of success. I had forgotten about Feudtner's work at the time, but looking back I wish someone had explicitly asked me to consider what my new, smaller hopes were.

There has been a great deal of research into the power and importance of hope for mental health over the last decade. For example, psychologists commonly recognise that hope counteracts mental illness and that hopeful individuals have a greater sense of meaning in life, and generally accomplish their goals more frequently, as well as doing better academically and in sports performance.[6] Rick Snyder and Shane Lopez, the academic partners leading this body of research, describe how by generating the motivation (the 'will power') and pathways (the 'way power') to get where we want to go, hope helps shape our lives and defines our goals. Very often the presence of hope makes all the difference between coping and depression.

Having goals is important; the absence of a goal is almost like depression—feeling listless, and lacking interest and a feeling of control over our actions. These are not goals like meeting deadlines; they're more about identifying what's important to you—the things you value. Doing so helps you focus where you put your energy, time and commitment; the things you chase, and the issues and complaints you let go.

What matters now may not be the same as what mattered to you before the death of your loved one. As one woman explained to me, 'Before my daughter's death I was obsessed with how the house looked and having everything in its right place. These things seem utterly irrelevant now.' Similarly, I read somewhere about a woman who, after the death of her husband, decided that what mattered now was staying healthy so that she could raise her children. She had previously cancelled two scheduled mammograms, but now she made sure she attended the appointments. Her motivations had changed, prompting a different course of action. Identifying your remaining or new, smaller hopes can be a worthwhile exercise.

Exercise in identifying hopes

Now that all hope of saving the person you love is gone, now that they are dead, what are you hoping for now?

Answering this question helps to identify the other, remaining hopes in life, and to in turn guide your decision-making. It helped me realise I did still have hope—multiple hopes, in fact. I hoped that we'd manage to survive this tragedy; that we'd stay sane; that we'd manage to remain a normal connected family; that my boys would be close friends and together cherish their little sister's memory. Identifying these other hopes has helped guide my decision-making over the past months.

Given what you are up against, what are you hoping for now?
What's important?
What's going on from your point of view?
If we decide to do _____, is this decision taking us closer to our true goals?
What things do matter to you now?
What can you do to help you get there?

Mindfulness

There's been a great deal of talk about mindfulness in recent years. It is a word that gets bandied about with good reason: mindfulness is a powerful force. Greater mindfulness has been shown to be associated with a host of desirable outcomes, from reduced stress, anxiety and depression, and increased longevity, to better physical health (including greater immunity and reduced pain), improved relationships and greater wellbeing.

Like resilience, mindfulness is a multi-dimensional, dynamic construct. Put more simply, there are many elements to mindfulness. While my academic training introduced me to the concept of mindfulness, it wasn't until the girls died that I truly came to understand its usefulness and particularly its relevance to grieving. Mindfulness is described in academic terms as 'the awareness that emerges through paying attention on purpose, in the present moment, and nonjudgmentally to the unfolding of experience moment by moment'.[7] In real life, that translates as being able to intentionally focus our attention, to fully attending to the present moment and successfully refraining from being easily distracted, and letting our thoughts wander aimlessly. Practising mindfulness is good for calming and focusing a racing mind. While mindfulness sits at the core of Buddha's teachings, it is neither a belief, nor an ideology, nor a philosophy. Rather, explains Jon Kabat-Zinn, Professor at the University of Massachusetts Medical School, there is nothing particularly Buddhist about it. 'We are all mindful to one degree or another, moment by moment. It is an inherent human capacity.'[8]

Although the best way to boost mindfulness is by developing a regular meditation practice (historically, mindfulness has been referred to as 'the heart' of Buddhist meditation), it doesn't have to involve meditation; we can all be more mindful in our everyday lives. In this sense, two types of mindfulness are recognised: formal mindfulness practice, which involves daily meditation and breathing exercises; and informal mindfulness practice, which involves bringing mindful attention to all aspects of our day-to-day lives. This means making an effort to be aware of our thoughts, emotions, feelings and the environment on a moment-to-moment basis, and to keep our minds focused on the present rather than wandering aimlessly.

NON-JUDGEMENTAL ACCEPTANCE OF THE MOMENT-BY-MOMENT EXPERIENCE? THAT'S MINDFULNESS.

In the work I do with organisations, I often find the best way to introduce the concept of mindfulness to a new audience is to consider it as the opposite of living mindlessly. Instead of running round like headless chickens, with our thoughts and attention scattered everywhere, living mindfully requires us to be aware of our thoughts and live our lives more intentionally. That doesn't mean we can never blob on the couch and zone out to watch TV again, just that we are consciously engaged with what we are choosing to do in our lives.

Mindfulness is a supportive tool for helping you live and in this sense it follows that it may be helpful during bereavement. Mindfulness will not make your grief disappear—no tool suggested in this book will do that—but it does 'provide a greater basket for tenderly holding and intimately knowing' pain.[9] In this way, mindfulness helped me accept my grief by allowing me to focus my attention on what I felt in any given moment, and to acknowledge that feeling in a non-judgemental fashion. In fact, it was only through grieving that I finally understood the non-judgemental aspect of mindfulness. To explain: instead of thinking 'Oh shoot, I'm crying again, in the middle of the supermarket, I'm such an idiot that I can't control my emotions, so weak for not being able to hold back the tears,' a more mindful me coaxed myself to think, 'Wow, here I go crying again, that's okay, it's just tears, the tears reflect the immense sadness I feel at Abi's loss, that's okay, it's just what they are and what you are feeling in this moment doesn't mean it will be forever, it's just here, right now.' Non-judgemental acceptance of the moment-by-moment experience? That's mindfulness.

Mindfulness also helped me overcome the fear of losing another child that threatened to consume me in the months after Abi's death. As we have seen, people who experience traumatic life events they could not control or prevent often report an increased sense of vulnerability. In the weeks immediately after the accident, as people came to the house to say their final goodbyes to Abi and surround us with love, a trickle of stories penetrated my protective cocoon. I heard of one friend who'd lost two siblings. Unthinkable. His mother had been fighting depression ever since. Another relayed the tragic story of his brother's loss, and while I'm ashamed to admit that I have forgotten the details of that death, I vividly recall reeling with dread at a follow-up comment describing how his other brother had been missing for many years now, presumably gone AWOL as a result of the tragedy. The thought that there might be more tragedy ahead tortured me. My knowledge of statistical probability didn't help: I was well aware that being unlucky once did nothing to reduce the likelihood of it happening again. Probability doesn't work like that. Every time I thought about it, my head swooned and I felt nauseous.

Looking back on it, I know that dealing with that vulnerability was one of the toughest challenges. To make matters worse, these were the months when our eldest son passed his driving test and was let loose on the open road. Unaccompanied. Oh, the agony. I knew I couldn't keep him back, and that worrying wasn't going to reduce his (and my) vulnerability. The only answer was mindfulness. And I found that continually drawing myself back to the present moment worked. Is it happening now? I'd ask myself. No, I'm fine, he's fine, we are all fine. If it happens, I'll deal with it then, but for now I'll keep in the present moment and deal with life experience as it unfolds before me. In my most anxious moments, this type of informal mindfulness and mindful breathing exercises like the ones set out below were the only things that kept me sane. Some of the new meditation apps, such as *1 Giant Mind* or *Headspace*, are also a good way of getting into the habit of meditating. These apps offer guided meditations which can help restore peace to the mind, and can be used very easily—even in the office at work (with headphones) or in the car.

MINDFUL BREATHING

Dr Elaine O'Brien acknowledges that she's struggled since her father died a few years back. 'One morning after a particularly rough bout of frustration,' she told me, 'I realised that my mouth was sore. I had been clenching my jaw overnight, possibly for hours. As a kinesiologist, looking at human movement psychology, I tend to be pretty attuned to my body; this was a completely new behaviour, which needed addressing immediately. One practice that has helped me minimise stress around my mouth is around mindful breathing.'

Outlined below are the breathing techniques that Dr O'Brien teaches and found useful for reducing the physical symptoms of her grief.

Begin with a neutral spine: crown of the head to the sky, ears over your shoulders, shoulders down and over your hips, tall neck, rib cage lifted, abdominals pulled in and up, knees slightly flexed, and the feet grounded into the earth.

Concentrate on:

- Your breath as it goes in and out of your nostrils—try not to breathe through your mouth.
- Your belly as it expands and contracts with the breath—you can put your hand on the belly to make it more real.
- Other parts of your body. This is an in-the-body rather that out-of-body experience. It is designed to make you aware of all bodily sensations.
- Sounds around you.
- Sights around you.
- A favourite mantra or word pair to utter to yourself silently as you inhale and exhale. Say one word to yourself slowly,

the whole time you inhale. Say the second word to yourself slowly as you exhale. (For example, inhale and say, *Here*, exhale and say, *Now*.)

- All breaths are executed with excellent posture, form, eyes open or closed, honouring the self and others.

Dr O'Brien suggests *5 Methods of Breathing*. Start with a deep exhalation; then breathe in fully through the nose, and out through the mouth, adopting the following patterns:

1. Complete breath/diaphragmatic breathing. Place one hand on your abdomen and the other on your upper chest. Slowly, and while visualising the lungs as three chambers, breathe in, and fill your belly, chest cavity and then the top of your lungs (by your collarbone, expanding the shoulders) with air. Exhale and repeat.

2. Rhythmic breathing and sigh of exhalation. Breathe in for a count of 4, hold the breath for a count of 7, and exhale audibly for a count of 8. Relax and repeat.

3. 1:2 ratio. Breathe in and out fully. Then breathe in for a count of 4, out for a count of 8. With practice, you can change the count to 5:10, or 6:12.

4. 5-to-1 count. Say and visualise the number '5' as you take a full deep breath in and out. Mentally count and visualise the number '4', saying to yourself, 'I am more relaxed than I was at 5.' Continue the countdown until you get to '1', and are totally relaxed.

5. Concentration breathing. Breathe in for 7 counts, hold for 7 counts, and exhale for 7 counts. Relax and repeat.

Dr Elaine O'Brien, personal communication, 10 November 2015.

Chapter 10

Relationships (and what friends and family can do to help)

AS HUMANS WE ARE hard wired for relationships, for connection with others.

Years ago, I was watching American TV show *Touch* and was sufficiently struck by the following words to rewind and write them down: 'Human beings are not the strongest species on the planet, not the fastest or the smartest. The one advantage we have is our ability to cooperate: to help each other out. We recognise ourselves in each other, we are programmed for compassion, for heroism, for love. And those things make us stronger, faster and smarter, that's why we survive.'

In grief, as in so many aspects of our lives (and particularly times of traumatic and adverse events), our relationships with others are vital. A large body of research has accumulated over the past three decades to indicate how important supportive relationships are for resilience. Numerous studies have shown that social support reduces psychological distress in the aftermath of trauma. For example, children who have best survived child poverty or abuse have usually done so because they found a supportive adult to help them through;[1] and adults exposed to trauma such as natural disaster, war and assault fare better if they are well supported.[2] Similarly, several studies have shown that people with strong social support networks are more unlikely to become depressed than those without such networks. Having even one supportive confidant reduced the risk of depression in half the research subjects following other painful events such as divorce or job loss.

SOCIAL SUPPORT REDUCES PSYCHOLOGICAL DISTRESS IN THE AFTERMATH OF TRAUMA.

Researchers at the Center on the Developing Child at Harvard University had this to say about resilience: 'There is no "resilience gene" that determines the life course of an individual irrespective of the experiences that shape genetic expression. The capacity to adapt and thrive despite adversity develops through the interaction of supportive relationships, gene expression, and adaptive biological systems. Despite the widespread belief that individual grit, extraordinary self-reliance, or some in-born, heroic strength of character can triumph over calamity, science now tells us that it is the reliable presence of at least one supportive relationship and multiple opportunities for developing effective coping skills that are the essential building blocks for the capacity to do well in the face of significant adversity.'[3]

As we have seen in Chapter 3, Charney and Southwick's interviews with American soldiers imprisoned during the Vietnam War reached the same conclusion. Very few individuals who have managed to demonstrate resilience in the face of trauma have done so alone. 'Everybody needs a tap code to get through tough times,' says Charney, referring to the POWs' habit of tapping through the alphabet so they could communicate even when detained in solitary confinement. 'You get enormous emotional strength from relationships and organisations such as MADD [Mothers Against Drunk Driving]. We know lots of advocacy organisations that help patients face cancer—these are incredibly important social networks that can be a safety net during times of stress.'[4]

A growing number of studies have indicated the importance of social support for successful grieving specifically. Even more sophisticated research methods have shown that certain types of social support are more useful to the bereaved than others. For instance, by studying the emotional wellbeing of recent widows, Toni Bisconti, Cindy Bergeman and Steven Boker revealed that widows seeking 'emotional support' adjusted more quickly to the loss than widows seeking 'instrumental support'.[5] In other words, in the early stages of bereavement, lending a sympathetic ear proved more helpful than mowing the grieving person's lawns.

Charney and Southwick's studies have indicated the tremendous influence role models can have for resilience. Several bereavement organisations have picked up on this, and now offer online and personal support for those who are grieving. For example, MotherLOVE connects newly bereaved mothers with those further down the track (www.motherlove.net) and the Modern Widows Club (www.modernwidowsclub.com) offers mentoring for widows. When I consider role models, I'm reminded of some lines from the reading my sister picked out for our mum's funeral. It comes from Albert Schweitzer, a German theologian, musician and medical missionary who was awarded the Nobel Peace Prize in 1952: 'I always think that we live, spiritually, by what others have given us in the significant hours of our life. These significant hours do not announce themselves as coming, but arrive unexpected. Nor do they make a great show of themselves; they pass almost unperceived. Often, indeed, their significance comes home to us first as we look back, just as the beauty of a piece of music or of a landscape often strikes us first in our recollection of it.'[6] I am reminded of this when I see people who were so significant during those life-changing hours of our life but now have resumed their normal roles. I know I'll never forget the kindness, compassion and generosity they demonstrated, on our behalf, at that vulnerable, terrible time. A tender connection exists with them that, even unspoken, acknowledges what we endured together.

The short story on resilience is that, in the words of one of my favourite professors, the late Chris Peterson, 'other people matter'. He used this phrase to summarise the findings of decades of research. Bereavement is something to be shared: we need others to discuss our feelings with, to talk openly with, to offer the veritable shoulder to cry on; we need others to keep memories of the dead alive; we need them to listen to us, cook for us, drive us places we cannot be bothered to go.

Our family, friends and wider communities have done so much to help us survive the grief. Living in a small coastal village, having struggled together through two years of successive earthquakes and the countless disruptions and losses associated with them, with our children having been through the local school, we, and Ella and Sally's family, were held, nurtured, and emotionally and practically supported throughout the weeks and months that followed the girls' deaths. This started the day after the accident, when our dear friend Victoria suggested we gather the girls' friends and families down at the beach so that the kids could comfort each other on hearing the news, and continued with a nightly roster of home-cooked meals for four *months*. Only when I was feeling stronger was this reduced to two nights a week for a further three months. All those meals, cooked and delivered with love—the women who organised it even developed a system for collecting and returning dishes. All we had to do was eat. Thank you, Kerm and Charlie. There was so much practical help: people lending cars for guests staying for the funeral, lots of visitors put up overnight or longer, a camper van delivered to our driveway for spillover guests, and the whole gang who stood up and made the funeral happen when it was something we could not even begin to contemplate. The emotional support is ongoing. I realise how lucky I am to live in a family-focused community where people feel the pain of our loss acutely, and inherently understand that it isn't something we will 'get over' soon. Their patience and willingness to come with us on this journey has been astonishing.

Being able to discuss concerns, losses and fears with people we love and trust can help lift us out of despair, as well as foster deeper connections. I read a piece in the *Guardian* online in 2015 in which a mother described the loss of her 36-year-old daughter, Kate Gross, to colon cancer, which Kate called 'the

WAYS THE BEREAVED CAN HELP OTHERS TO SUPPORT THEM THROUGH GRIEF

Tell them what you need

Don't expect people to be mind-readers. You know they can't possibly understand what you are feeling. Imagining your friends and family are mind-readers is known in psychology as a 'thinking trap', and is recognised as a significant barrier to resilience. Fortunately, it's relatively easy to overcome. All we have to do is assist our friends by (gently) telling them what we need. Most, with a little steering in the right direction, will prove worthy companions and supporters if given a nudge in the right direction. Tell them if you need a hug, don't want to be hugged, need air in your car tyres, could do with someone to attend the school play with, to babysit your kids, to help you make decisions about your loved one's clothes. Ask yourself, have I made my feelings or beliefs known directly and clearly? Am I expecting the other person to work hard at figuring out my needs?

Tell the truth

Try to be as open with your feelings as possible, even if they are hard to articulate. Even if they change every minute, tell those closest to you. Explain to them that when you say you are fine, you're not, but that it's hard to know how to encapsulate the torrid emotional journey that is grieving in a one-line answer to the question 'How are you doing?' In the book she wrote in response to her daughter's death, Sandy Fox suggests we say, 'I'm doing the best I can.'[7] That seems a reasonable goal and a succinct reply that doesn't claim we're sailing through.

Don't feel guilty/ashamed about laughing in front of others

Some bereaved people have expressed concerns over this, feeling that their loved ones may take laughter as a sign that they a) have recovered or b) do not respect the dead. In fact, people who do manage to laugh and display positive emotions around others cope better with grief. As explained in Chapter 7, sharing good moments with our friends helps keep those connections with others healthy.

Address the elephant in the room (particularly at work)

While we may think that avoiding discussing the death at work is the best plan, my conversations with the bereaved indicate that it rarely is. Sheryl Sandberg, Chief Operating Officer of Facebook, says that on returning to work after the death of her husband, she felt compelled to address the elephant in the room. 'Many of my co-workers had a look of fear in their eyes as I approached. I knew why—they wanted to help but weren't sure how. I realised that to restore the closeness with my colleagues that has always been so important to me, I needed to let them in. And that meant being more open and vulnerable than I ever wanted to be. I told those I work with most closely that they could ask me their honest questions and I would answer. I also said it was okay for them to talk about how they felt. Speaking openly replaced the fear of doing and saying the wrong thing . . . Once I addressed the elephant, we were able to kick him out of the room.'[8] Allowing people to talk about your loss seems to let everyone behave more normally.

Nuisance'. 'It has helped to have the love of family and friends, and the kindness of strangers, the thousands of messages we have received. Because of the Nuisance, we became a much closer family. We bridged the distances that grow between parents and their adult children and came to know and admire Kate and Jo, much more than we would have otherwise. We became part of Oscar and Isaac's daily lives instead of occasional visitors. And we were—and still are—overwhelmed at the way Kate's friends and our own have responded to her illness. I've learned that there is more love in the world than I ever knew and that perhaps all we need to do is learn to ask for what we need,' wrote Jean Gross.[9]

Her words hold an essential key to grief: that we cannot expect others to know instinctively how to help us, what to say, what to do, when to call and when to leave us alone. If we want them to understand and respect that grieving is an individual process, then they need our help; they need us to guide them and tell them what we need. People are always asking me what helps, what doesn't? In answer to those two questions and following a request from my friend Georgie, below is a list of both.

What can family, friends and colleagues do to help?

Watching loved ones grieve is a painful process that often makes us feel excruciatingly helpless. What friends can do to help depends, of course, on the particular circumstances of the bereaved—who they lost, how it happened, who is left in their lives, and so on. People often respond and relate differently to friends, family members, acquaintances and colleagues in the aftermath of death. Sometimes a friend's grief can trigger off your own grief experience as you remember those you've lost. Try not to burden them with this, but to be there for them and listen to their grief story and needs.

The most important thing to understand, counsels Thomas Attig, is that each bereavement is different, so try to focus your energies on intently listening to and endeavouring to understand (and accept) their story of their grief. Above all he urges patient, active listening, focused on acknowledging the personal nature and individual differences of the person's loss and reassuring them that you will stand by them as long as it takes.[10]

1. Let the bereaved tell their story

One of the first requirements of healthy grieving is to accept that the loss has occurred. Friends and relatives can help with this by allowing the bereaved to talk. Going over the details of a loved one's death helps the reality of it sink in.

Even now, when given the chance, I gain some satisfaction or relief from talking about the night we heard about the girls' accident, going over events again, re-living certain aspects. For some odd reason, I sometimes also like to hear how others found out about the accident, and ask, 'Where were you, who told you?' Apparently, regurgitating the story of our loss helps relieve the pain. I suspect that hearing how painful the news was to them, how much it shocked them too, validates my own pain, reassuring me of the totally unexpected and profoundly terrible nature of their deaths. Hearing their memories tells me, 'Yes, it really was that bad, which is why it's so hard for you to come to terms with it.' It is a primal part of the grieving process. According to Kübler-Ross and Kessler, 'You must get it out. Grief must be witnessed to be healed. Grief shared is grief abated. Tell your tale, because it reinforces that your loss mattered.' For this reason, support from friends and family is essential, and their patience is definitely required. 'In sharing our story, we dissipate the pain little by little, giving a small drop to those we meet to disperse it along the way,' they add. 'When someone is telling you their story over and over, they are trying to figure something out. There has to be a missing piece or they too would be bored. Rather than rolling our eyes and saying "there she goes again", ask questions about parts that don't connect. Be the witness and even the guide. Look for what they want to know.'[11]

Be a patient listener and encourage the bereaved to talk about the loss (if they show signs of wanting to do so). Ask:

- *Where did the death occur?*
- *Where were you when you were told about it?*
- *Who were you with?*
- *What was the funeral like?*
- *Who spoke at the service?*
- *Was your loved one buried or cremated?*
- *Where are they buried?*
- *Where are the ashes?*
- *Do you visit the grave or the site of the ashes?*

Another way to help cement that the death has actually occurred is to offer to visit the grave with the bereaved. Be sensitive—they may prefer to go on their own—but tell them you'd always be happy to accompany them any time, and (because you don't want to keep pestering them about it) you'll leave it up to them to ask you if they ever think that would be helpful.

Other useful questions:

- *What works for you?*
- *How do you react when . . . ?*
- *Have your feelings changed?*
- *What are your most difficult times?*
- *Do you feel like talking about it today?*

2. Help the bereaved adjust (practically) to life without their loved one

Anyone who has lost a partner will be coming to terms not only with emotional turmoil but also with the loss of all the roles played by the deceased. Everything from cooking to putting out the rubbish/recycling, dealing with school teachers, paying the bills, buying a car, booking holidays, backing the trailer and doing the washing commonly get departmentalised in relationships, leaving us bereft when the partner who took care of these practical, and often everyday, tasks is no longer with us. Ask yourself:

- *What are the practical challenges the survivor faces and how can you help to solve any of them?*
- *Who was the decision-maker in their relationship?*
- *What decisions (big or small) are worrying them most now, and with whom might they like to talk these things over?*

3. Discourage the bereaved from making major life-changing decisions too soon

Grieving is hard enough: it's better done in a familiar environment, and decisions are best not undertaken while grieving. Worden cautions: 'In discouraging the bereaved from making major life-changing decisions too soon, be careful that you are not promoting a sense of helplessness. Rather, communicate that they will be quite capable of making decisions and taking actions when they are ready and that they should not make decisions just to reduce the pain.'[12]

4. Help the bereaved reminisce

A massive challenge for the bereaved involves letting go of that old life while simultaneously getting on with embracing the new one. It is quite normal during this time for the bereaved to worry that they and others will forget their loved ones. I know I struggled to hear Abi's voice, even to picture her face at times. But, having lost my mother 13 years earlier, I also knew that these things do come back.

Supporters can play an important role here, reassuring the bereaved that their memories will not fade, that their loved one will never be forgotten. We are all a product of our experiences, and memories of these experiences don't die just because those involved are no longer alive. Some people find it hard (or even distasteful) to talk about the dead; some avoid bringing the subject up for fear of upsetting the bereaved by making them think of the loved one. I hope I'm correct in saying that no one who is bereaved will ever mind you talking about those they loved. As for not upsetting me by making me think about Abi, Ella and Sally, I'm thinking about them all the time anyway, so go ahead and join me.

In this sense, supporters can help the grieved by sharing their own memories of the dead. You can also:

- recall humorous moments, events, and expressions
- specifically list the qualities of the dead that you recognised and valued

- post a picture on Instagram or Facebook, accompanied by your version of #abiwouldhavelovedthis when something reminds you of the deceased, or you see/do something you know they would have loved. I came across this idea on the What's Your Grief website (www.whatsyourgrief.com) which has lots of useful resources, blogs and insights on grieving.

5. Understand the bereaved lack tolerance for life's small frustrations/details

When someone you love dies, the world stops. Nothing else matters. I remember staring at all the magazines on sale in the supermarket after my mother died, wondering why anyone would be interested in such trivia.

In the immediate aftermath of Abi's death, we were constantly amazed at how tolerant everyday life requires us to be. And how little tolerance we had now that such enormous issues faced us. Our friends assisted us hugely here—paving the way or taking over when we were confronted with a challenging situation that they instinctively knew would test our patience. For instance, I recall my work colleague Kate helping me out one day at the local pool. We both had pre-paid entry tickets which we'd topped up the week before but, for some odd reason, mine was indicating I had no swims left. 'You go and get changed, I'll deal with this,' she said, ushering me towards the changing room, knowing that I'd bolt with very little provocation rather than endure a protracted negotiation.

6. Give the bereaved time to grieve

It might be a cliché but grieving takes time, and the best support networks for the bereaved are those people who truly understand this.

Keep reminding the bereaved you haven't forgotten their pain and you don't expect them to be 'over it'. My dear friend Toni continues to show her empathy to Trevor and me by randomly texting us emoji hearts. For the first year after Abi died, she sent one every day, just to let us know that she was thinking of us. After the first anniversary of Abi's death, she just kept going, not every day, but intermittently. Small acts like this can mean a great deal.

Also bear in mind that some specific time points are going to be worse than others. Check in around the three-month mark, when counsellors are often told by the bereaved that no one seems to care anymore and people are avoiding them. The first anniversary and all birthdays and holidays are also particularly difficult. These are times to offer additional support or just a friendly text or email to show you are aware and they are not forgotten.

7. Don't compare your own grief stories with those of the very recently bereaved

Although the bereaved often become very empathetic listeners, supporting other bereaved, this can take time. When a friend, colleague or family member has newly lost someone they love, the immediate aftermath is not an appropriate time to compare your own grief experiences. Best option is often, 'I just don't know what to say to you', or 'I can't imagine how tough it is.' The following poem says it so well.

. . . .

Just Say You Are Sorry

Please don't ask me if I'm over it yet.
I'll never be over it.
Please don't tell me she's in a better place.
She isn't with me.
Please don't say at least she isn't suffering.
I haven't come to terms with why she had to suffer
    at all.
Please don't tell me you know how I feel,
Unless you have lost a child.
Please don't ask me if I feel better.
Bereavement isn't a condition that clears up.
Please don't tell me at least you had her for so
    many years.
What year would you choose for your child to die?
Please don't tell me God never gives us more than
    we can bear.
Please just say you are sorry.
Please just say you remember my child, if you do.
Please just let me talk about my child.
Please mention my child's name.
Please just let me cry.[13]

Rita Moran, 'Just Say You Are Sorry', 1999.

. . . .

8. Stand by through depression

Depression is a common (but usually temporary) symptom of grief, as people grow to accept the reality of their loss. People often seem to want to cajole the bereaved out of depression, to cheer them up, but what we really need is friends to stand quietly by us and understand that it's part of the process. Sit with us and accept that we are profoundly sad and that we may need life to just slip quietly by us for a little while.

You might also like to suggest that you're happy to support the bereaved in doing regular exercise. Physical exercise is itself a mood booster; but people will often need encouragement and assistance in making this a regular part of their day. There is more on the importance of exercise in Chapter 13.

INAPPROPRIATE THINGS TO SAY TO THE BEREAVED

- *At least she's in a better place now.* Better? Really? She liked it here, on earth, living with us and all her friends.
- *Are you feeling better yet?* It's not a disease; it's not something I'm going to 'get over' because it's not temporary.
- *I know how you feel—my dog/hamster died last year.* No comment.
- *Everything happens for a reason.* 'Let me be crystal clear: if you've faced a tragedy and someone tells you in any way, shape or form that your tragedy was meant to be, that it happened for a reason, that it will make you a better person, or that taking responsibility for it will fix it, you have every right to remove them from your life,' writes blogger Tim Lawrence.[14] For the record, let me also be crystal clear: I also don't believe everything happens for a reason. I don't believe I am a *better* person because I've had to change my life as a result of losing Abi; I'm not trying to coerce you into becoming a better person via the strategies in this

book either. I merely believe that, faced with circumstances beyond my control, I've been forced to take a new life path, to relearn the world. Do I welcome it? No. Has finding new directions helped me get through the pain and emptiness of losing my daughter? Yes.

- *You'll be united up in heaven.* If you're going to say this, please be sure the person believes this. I (sadly) don't, so this offers me no comfort at all. Instead, I really have to accept that Abi is gone forever and that I'm not going to see her again. Along the same lines, there's something profoundly inappropriate and irritating about teenagers' posts asking 'Are you having fun up there in heaven Abi?' on Instagram or Facebook.
- *It'll be okay.* I kind of know it will, but I don't want this to be okay.

Non-supportive behaviours:
- changing the subject
- talking too much about yourself
- asking 'why' questions
- preaching or lecturing
- asking too many questions.

HOW TO TALK TO CHILDREN ABOUT DEATH (BY LISA BUKSBAUM)

Despite feeling apprehensive when talking to children about death, we need to support children through difficult times in order to facilitate healing.

- Let your children be your guide. If you don't know what they know or understand about the death, ask open-ended questions to see what they know and what questions they may have. Let your child's questions and responses guide you as to how much information to provide. Give children ample opportunity over time to ask questions.

- Let your children know you are there for them and ready to listen.

- Never try to 'fix it' or justify the death.

- Be honest with your children. Give them clear and honest answers to their questions. Children want, need and deserve the truth and need to know they can trust you to tell them the truth. You may worry that you won't know what to say or have all the answers. It is okay to say, 'I don't know', or 'I don't understand that either'.

- Listen to your children when they are not talking. *Know that your children are listening to you when you are talking.* Children will not always talk about their feelings directly, but you can learn a lot by paying attention to their play, what they are saying while playing, what they are drawing or writing. Children see, hear, feel and absorb what goes on around them. You may think your children are not listening, but they hear you when you are in conversation with others, or on the phone. Children have built-in radar.

- Acknowledge your children's feelings. Let children know that any feelings they may be having are okay and normal. Help your child label their feelings (such as 'sad', 'angry', 'frustrated' or 'overwhelmed').

- Assure your child. Be sure to clarify any misconceptions or misinformation. Remind your child that people care about them and will help keep them safe.
- Model for your children. Show children how you appropriately express your emotions and take care of yourself during the grief process. It is okay to let your child see how you feel, but do not use your child as your support system. Rely on other adults or professionals for your emotional support.
- Look for changes in your child's behaviour. Changes may be a sign that they are feeling upset or unsettled. Be aware of changes in eating, sleeping, playing or the ability to concentrate. If your child's usual behaviour continues to be disrupted, contact a professional for support.
- There is comfort in keeping to normal routines and schedules. Stick to normal routines as much as possible. Continue with regular schedules of sleeping, eating, school, extra-curricular activities and play time with friends. These routines give your child a sense of security.
- Not all children will understand death the same way.

Young children—do not understand that death is permanent. They may ask the same questions again and again. This repetition helps them process and understand what has happened. Keep explanations short and simple and reassure them that they are cared for and safe. Young children will absorb and mimic your stress and feelings.

School-age children—are better able to understand what has happened and that death is permanent. They may have unrealistic reactions to death, may blame themselves for what has happened or worry that others will die. Provide honest facts and information about the death. Help them express themselves through art or writing and help them label their feelings such as 'sad', 'stress', 'overwhelmed'.

Adolescents—may have the same understanding of death as adults have though perhaps not the experience with death and grief. Give adolescents time and space to work out their feelings. Allow them their privacy, but don't let them withdraw too much. Involve them in decisions and conversations about the death. Let them know you are available if they need to talk. Help them figure out what they can do that is meaningful to them. They may want to channel them into a community project or some act of charity so they feel like they are taking a positive action.

It is helpful to invite children of all ages to write or draw their positive feelings and memories about the person who has died. Open-ended questions such as, 'What are some of your favourite memories with this person?' or 'What is the thing you are most grateful to have shared with this person?' are ways in which children can express themselves and build memories about the person who died.

Lisa Buksbaum is the CEO & founder of Soaringwords, a non-profit charity devoted to helping millions of ill children and their families to heal. She started the organisation after three experiences with death and illness in her family. To date it has helped 250,000 children and families to 'Never give up!' Visit www.soaringwords.org

Exercise in reaching out to others

1. Name three people you feel comfortable talking to.
2. How often in the past week have you talked to each of them?
3. What practical step can you take to see or talk with each of the three more?
4. Name the number one person you feel comfortable expressing sad feelings to.
5. Think of one more person you currently don't express sad feelings to, but whom you think would make a good listener.
6. What practical step can you take to enable you to talk to this person? Does it require a dedicated time, a specific environment, finding a place where you won't be interrupted?
7. Name three people who help promote positive emotions in you.
8. Work out one way to see each of these people over the next three weeks (ask them to help you make a plan that appeals).

Chapter 11

Strengths

RESILIENCE SCIENTISTS STRESS the importance of understanding and harnessing our personal strengths to weather adverse events. One of the basic tenets of the relatively new academic disciplines of wellbeing and resilience science is that they adopt a strengths-based approach. Whereas psychology has traditionally adopted a deficit-based stance, focusing on identifying and treating mental illness (fixing what is wrong with people), resilience psychology focuses on a range of personal strengths that assist healthy adaptation to trauma.

To enable sound empirical research investigating associations between character strengths and life satisfaction, occupational and educational performance, and physical health, psychologists first had to devise a classification system and methods to measure those strengths. In the early 2000s, 55 distinguished scientists therefore worked together on a three-year project to create a classification of positive human traits. The resulting Values in Action (VIA) classification of character strengths, comprising 24 universally valued different strengths of character, has since been employed by scientists in hundreds of peer-reviewed studies conducted across cultures.[1]

Strengths, in this context, mean 'positive traits reflected in thoughts, feelings, and behaviours'.[2] We all have strengths, but each of us rates ourselves as stronger in some and weaker in others.

Like most people, I wasn't aware of possessing any particular character strengths until I took the VIA survey as part of my training. A quick (around five minutes) online psychological survey determines your leading strengths of character and delivers them to you in an email—it's as easy as that. Go to www.viacharacter. org or see the box at the end of this chapter. To date 2.6 million people across 190 countries have taken the survey.

Studies show that knowing our strengths is associated with a raft of desirable outcomes—including academic and career success, achieving personal goals, higher performance at work, and better health. But when I conducted my own empirical research into character strengths, I was still surprised by the results. Because my work frequently involves assisting businesses to develop and implement wellbeing and resilience strategies, I was interested to investigate what impact using strengths had in the workplace. I was fortunate enough, working at Auckland University of Technology, to have access to a sizeable database of New Zealand workers who had all responded to the *Sovereign Wellbeing Index, New Zealand's First National Wellbeing Survey*. By analysing the responses to scores of questions on wellbeing, I was able to split the large sample of workers (over 5000 adults) into two groups—those who were really flourishing in life (according to a whole battery of psychological variables) and those who were languishing. The results showed that those employees reporting that they knew their strengths were eight times more likely to be psychologically flourishing than those who seldom used their strengths. Moreover, once I took the analysis a stage further to explore the impact of employees actually using their strengths, I found that those using their strengths most were 18 times more likely to experience flourishing mental health than those seldom using their strengths. What's more, this result was independent of socio-demographic differences and participants' income. This was a staggering finding.

KNOWING OUR STRENGTHS IS ASSOCIATED WITH A RAFT OF DESIRABLE OUTCOMES.

Having said this, I wasn't particularly aware of having harnessed the power of my strengths during the first six months of bereavement until I was asked to present my work at an academic conference. Once I sat down and carefully considered if and where I'd used any of the VIA character strengths to aid my recovery, I was surprised to discover how much I had leaned on them for support and direction at different times.

Prior to Abi's death, I knew that the character strengths I related to most (my 'Signature Strengths' in VIA parlance), and that were consistently identified when I did the survey, were love, gratitude, enthusiasm, perseverance, curiosity and love of learning. From previous assessments, I was also aware that forgiveness, honesty and bravery were way down my list—strengths I did not view as essential parts of my character. So, it struck me as ironic that, at the darkest juncture of my life, forgiveness was the character strength that came to my rescue. As a researcher investigating character strengths I should not have been so surprised, given that 'we may all possess strengths that we do not display until we are truly challenged'.[3] Apparently, crises do not necessarily forge character, but reveal it. Psychologists call this the Truman Effect, after the incredible transformation displayed by Harold Truman who went from living an undistinguished life to becoming a great American president in the wake of Roosevelt's death.

Forgiveness came quickly and naturally to us. From the night we were told about Abi's death, all four of us agreed that we wouldn't blame the driver. It wasn't that we *didn't* recognise the driver's culpability. Given he ran straight through a STOP sign on a rural Canterbury road to hit the car Abi was in, we were all too aware that he was in the wrong. It was more that we instinctively knew no good would come from blaming him. It was not a wrong that could be righted—at least not in any way we wanted. Nothing was going to bring her back. Forgiveness was the only logical choice: in the face of so much pain, misery and loss, what possible benefit could be gained from not forgiving him? I was already pretty sure he was unlikely to ever do it again.

Forgiveness also provided something of an aligning framework for us in those first few days and weeks. No one else in my family would outwardly acknowledge the impact of our collective forgiveness (that's just the role of the overly psychologically aware mother!), but the unifying bond it offered us is perhaps best understood by imagining the discord that would have reigned had three of us felt forgiving and one cast blame towards the driver. That dissonance would have brought a very different atmosphere to our household indeed.

'TO ALL THE PEOPLE OUT THERE WHO FEEL ANGER FOR THE MAN WHO HIT THEM, DO NOT': FACEBOOK POST FROM ED HONE, AGED 16

You all will probably know of the occurrences of the last few days by now. This is without a doubt the worst thing that has ever happened to our families.

Words cannot do justice to the pain, irregularity, loneliness, loss and love that losing our little Abi, the lovely Ella and one of the most kind, giving and approachable Mums that Sally was.

The last few days have been seriously rough in the Hone house. Moods swinging from beautiful happiness, to unspeakable sadness, and the most odd feeling of normality.

I don't think it has quite set in yet, no one is ready to believe that we could have lost three of the most important people in our lives in one swift, sudden and final hit. It is easy to contemplate the obscene amount of coincidences that have to occur in the right order at the right time, in the right place to the right people in order for a car crash to occur. It is easy to think that maybe if I'd said that last word to Abi before she left the car that morning, that car would have missed them.

In some words it is 'The Perfect Storm', an inconceivably perfect accident that is comparable with the natural disaster that was the earthquakes which we endured only a short time ago. For this 'Perfect Storm' to occur countless things must happen in the perfect order, but we also must realise that it is this concept which makes the perfect storm so unlikely and that it does not occur more often. However, this perfect storm took three of our finest. It is also easy to simply shift our blame and anger to the driver of the vehicle that hit them. This is not only completely inhuman and wrong but also completely insensitive. To all the people out there who feel anger for the man who hit them, do not. The fact of the matter is, that man did not get out of bed that day and say to himself that he was going to murder three people. If you blame him then you simply do not get it. Everyone has to understand that the man will be feeling every bit as hurt as we all are.

When you see these kind of things happening to people in the news, on TV, in the paper, never once, not even once does the thought possibly cross your mind that something like this would happen to someone you know, let alone someone you are related to, let alone your own sister or mum. But in reality as Rufus [Ed's cousin] put it on the night of the accident, 'Life Happens'. Along with other wise words from Rufus which comforted the family that evening. The most important thing in times like these is that we all stick together.

Gratitude has always played a big role in my life. I have a habit developed over the years of appraising my life and feeling extremely grateful for all that I have. Abi had it too: she used to literally shake with the thrill of all that she had—something I remember doing as a child. Initially, this habit worked against me in bereavement, because it made me constantly aware how awful my life had become. But gratitude has returned over time. I have been able to firmly ring-fence Abi's death and choose to focus on the good aspects of her life instead. I often find myself

thinking how lucky we were to have had her alive for *all* of the boys' childhood, so that, in time, I hope we will be able to look back on their childhood years with our family intact, enjoying unblemished memories quite separate from her premature death. Gratitude also helps draw my focus back towards the boys and all that we have, rather than dwelling exclusively on what we have lost.

Love is my backstop, some kind of cure-all, a salve for all woes. When misery bites, I have turned to love to pull me back into the world and to switch my focus. Our capacity for love amazes me. Enhanced empathy is recognised as a frequent by-product of losing someone we love. Bereavement makes us acutely aware how important relationships are: how fragile and precious too. I certainly feel less judgemental, more accepting and kinder than I was before the accident. Besides, actively helping others gives us a break from the obsession with our own loss and pain. I can recall walking and talking with friends, asking about their lives over that first year, being told, 'You don't want to hear about my troubles though', and explaining that yes, actually, I do. It helps to look beyond my own reduced world. But, bearing in mind what I said in the previous chapter about how frustrating it can be when others compare their grief to our new fresh experience, there's obviously a fine line to be trod here. Sometimes hearing about and sharing in others' worlds can be most therapeutic for the bereaved; I guess the trick is to take their cue.

Over the past year, my **curiosity** and **love of learning** has propelled my quest for knowledge about grief and bereavement. I've read endlessly, soaking up all the research, blogs, poetry and personal accounts I can in the hope of finding answers—to grow my understanding of the processes of grief, find the missing pieces of the jigsaw puzzle and take solace from shared experience. Knowing that others have felt and experienced the same really has helped—making me feel less alone, and, quite frankly, less mad.

Others I have spoken with while researching this book have shared stories of the changes they've noticed in their character as a result of their loss, and the strengths that have supported them along their journey through grief. For example, my colleague Dr Elaine O'Brien says that 'learning about, identifying, and applying VIA character strengths has been an important tool in helping me cope with bereavement and losses in my life'.[4] She gives the following examples of how bravery, kindness, humour, gratitude and spirituality helped her.

Bravery, she said, 'was important for me to be a vigilant, vocal advocate for our family when all my father's bodily systems seemed to be shutting down. Against my father's verbal wishes for wanting to "rest", his medical team let him down, just torturing him, giving him procedure after procedure. I spoke up for what I believed my father wanted, but this was all too often met with deaf ears from the doctors. Even after my father's death, I continued to advocate, writing letters to the hospital about their poor care and communications, as well as aiming to advocate for people to start discussions about end of life wishes and conversations. I would not want others to experience what our family, and especially my father, had experienced.

'Seeing the **kindness** and care my husband, Sean, demonstrated toward my father always, but especially after he was "locked in" and could not speak from a stroke, made me fall in love with him all over again. The care my daughter, Lianna, showed for me during the losses of both my parents' abilities was a comfort, and made me proud of her grace and kind-heartedness. Realising the power of giving, and receiving, comfort and care from those who care about me, and my family, truly lifted my spirits during times of despair. Having **humour** in your back pocket, and remembering friends who really enjoyed life, inspired me and lifted me up when I felt there was no feeling of hope or joy.

'Learning about **spiritual practices** across cultures, exploring different ways of honouring, revering, and remembering, along with the recitation of prayers from childhood provided me with comfort during dark hours.'

Indeed, there's good evidence to show that attending religious services is strongly related with resilience.[5] Although religion isn't for everyone, it's easy to see how being part of a religious group gives support and a strong sense of purpose in life. Having a set of beliefs that very few experiences can shatter is a frequent theme in resilience research. As Charney points out, these don't have to be religious beliefs: 'For many of the people we've met it was faith in the traditional sense, being religious, but in others it was a non-religious but important spiritual belief, or having a moral compass or a purpose in life that helps you get through tough times.'[6]

IDENTIFY YOUR SIGNATURE STRENGTHS

While studies show that character strengths help to buffer against stress and improve coping ability, there has not been much research specifically investigating how character strengths assist grieving. So, in the interests of conducting my own research experiment, I decided to re-do the VIA Character Strengths survey, according to how useful the 24 strengths had proved towards my grieving.

The best way to do this assessment is to go online to www.viacharacter.org. By entering this book's unique identifier code (NGNL11), you will be contributing to my research into the association between character strengths and grief. This will in no way compromise your anonymity. The good people at the Values in Action Institute maintain strict codes of scientific ethics, so they will just be supplying me with raw scores in an Excel spreadsheet which prevents individuals from being identified.

For a less scientific (but more immediate) alternative, follow these instructions.

STEP 1

Looking at the list of strengths below, rate each one on a 1–10 basis, where 1 is 'I haven't used this strength while grieving' to 10: 'this strength has been essential to my grieving'. Try to be honest and score them according to how you are, not how you'd like to be! Write a score next to each strength.

Creativity (originality, ingenuity): thinking of novel and productive ways to conceptualise and do things; this includes, but is not limited to, artistic achievement.

Curiosity (interest, novelty-seeking, openness to experience): taking an interest in ongoing experience for its own sake; finding subjects and topics fascinating; continually exploring and discovering.

Judgement (critical thinking): thinking things through and examining them from all sides; not jumping to conclusions; being able to change your mind in light of evidence; weighing up all the evidence fairly.

Love of learning: mastering new skills, topics and bodies of knowledge, whether on your own or through formal instruction; obviously related to the strength of curiosity but goes beyond it to describe the tendency to add systematically to what you know.

Perspective (wisdom): being able to provide wise counsel to others; having ways of looking at the world that make sense to you and to other people.

Bravery (valour): not shrinking from threat, challenge, difficulty, or pain; speaking up for what is right even in the presence of opposition; acting on convictions even if unpopular; includes physical bravery but is not limited to it.

Perseverance (persistence, industriousness): finishing what you start; persisting in a course of action in spite of obstacles; 'getting it out the door'; taking pleasure in completing tasks.

Honesty (authenticity, integrity): speaking the truth but more broadly presenting yourself in a genuine way and acting sincerely; being without pretence; taking responsibility for your feelings and actions.

Zest (vitality, enthusiasm, vigour, energy): approaching life with excitement and energy; not doing things half-heartedly; living life as an adventure; feeling alive and activated.

Love: valuing close relations with others, in particular those in which sharing and caring are reciprocated; being close to people.

Kindness (generosity, nurturance, care, compassion, altruistic love): doing favours and good deeds for others; helping them and taking care of them.

Social intelligence (emotional intelligence, personal intelligence): being aware of the motives and feelings of yourself and others; knowing what to do to fit into different social situations; knowing what makes other people tick.

Teamwork (citizenship, social responsibility, loyalty): working well as a member of a group or team; being loyal to the group; doing your share.

Fairness: treating all people the same according to notions of fairness and justice; not letting personal feelings bias decisions about others; giving everyone a fair chance.

Leadership: encouraging a group, of which you are a member, to get things done, and at the same time maintaining good relations within the group; organising group activities and ensuring they happen.

Forgiveness: forgiving those who have done wrong; accepting the shortcomings of others; giving people a second chance; not being vengeful.

Humility: letting your accomplishments speak for themselves; not regarding yourself as special.

Prudence: being careful about your choices; not taking undue risks; not saying or doing things that might later be regretted.

Self-regulation (self-control): regulating your feelings and actions; being disciplined; controlling your appetite and emotions, overcoming short-term desires for long-term benefit.

Appreciation of beauty and excellence (awe, wonder, elevation): noticing and appreciating beauty, excellence, and/or skilled performance in various domains of life, from nature to art to mathematics to science, to everyday experience.

Gratitude: being aware of and thankful for the good things that happen; taking time to express thanks.

Hope (optimism, future-mindedness, future orientation): expecting the best in the future and working to achieve it; believing that a good future is something that can be brought about.

Humour (playfulness): liking to laugh and tease; bringing smiles to other people; seeing the light side; making (not necessarily telling) jokes.

Spirituality (faith, purpose): having coherent beliefs about the higher purpose and meaning of the universe; knowing where you fit in the larger scheme of life; having beliefs about the meaning of life that shape conduct and provide comfort.

• •

STEP 2

Looking at the strengths with the Top 5 scores, ask yourself the following questions to identify your 'Signature Strengths'.

Is this the real me?
Do I enjoy using this strength?
Does using this strength energise me?

Write your Top 5 Signature Strengths here:

1. _____

2. _____

3. _____

4. _____

5. _____

Pick one of your Signature Strengths and try to use it more over the next week.

Ask yourself the following questions:

How did you find this exercise?
What did you learn by filling out this survey?
Are some of these strengths more useful while grieving than others?
Which ones?
Did you score much higher or lower on one strength than you anticipated?

How does _____ strength feel for you when
you use it?

Who sees this strength in you?

What about your partner, what strengths do you see in them?

Are there some strengths you consider as family strengths?

When have you used this strength in the past?

How might you apply these strengths to help in your grief?

Where else in your life could you use these strengths now?

Chapter 12

Managing exhaustion and depression through rest and exercise

GRIEF IS UTTERLY EXHAUSTING. Nine months in I went back to sleeping in the afternoons whenever I could. Partly due to the pointlessness of it all, but usually just due to plain old tiredness. Grief is so unlike any other of life's challenges. I have found myself bewildered and frustrated by the never-ending nature of it all. Usually, when I have a job to do, I work out a plan of how to get through it and, eventually, with enough hard graft, problem-solving and continual effort, reach the end. Job done, take a break, start again. But with grieving it feels as though there is no end, no break. Just one perpetual uphill struggle to convince yourself this is do-able: up, up, up we go, and instead of being rewarded with a downhill cruise after all the effort, along comes another hill. Some days it's a hill, others a mountain, at times you find yourself in a lull of acceptance—a gully between the uphill slogs. But up you have to go, again and again. No wonder it's exhausting.

Successful grieving requires successful energy management. For me, this started with acknowledging my tiredness to myself, and then to others. Now Trevor and I have conversations about tiredness over and over again, particularly on Monday mornings, which are always the worst.

'Think I must have some kind of virus,' he'll say.

'Maybe. More likely it's just the exhausting process of grieving and living without her,' I'll reply.

SUCCESSFUL GRIEVING REQUIRES SUCCESSFUL ENERGY MANAGEMENT.

Having acknowledged it ourselves, the importance of letting other people know also became clear. If I hadn't told others how frequently I felt tired, they might have thought us rude for leaving parties, work or work functions early. Rude, or lightweight, or uncommitted. Telling them that, even nine months later, I often felt overwhelmingly tired and just needed to bail out or have a 20-minute power nap in the car, or on the couch in the office, helped me from feeling bad or becoming overwhelmed. As I've said before, part of my ground rules for trying to return as quickly as possible to regular functioning is that I do not ignore the signs of my grief when they require my attention. The graphic below outlines the steps to take.

Acknowledge your tiredness to yourself—grief is exhausting, this is normal	→	Tell others— they're not mind-readers, tell them how you feel	→	Be realistic with what you can achieve/do	→	Work out times for sleep/recovery— 'the power nap', weekend rules

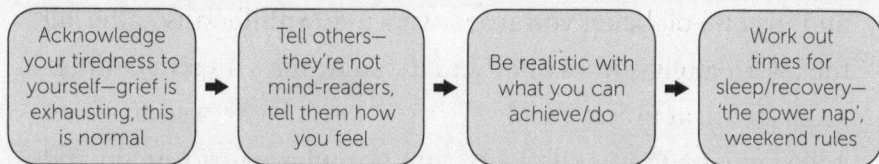

Grief is also exhausting because there's no way to get away from it. How many of us have booked a holiday or just a weekend elsewhere to have a break, only to discover that grief knows no geographical boundaries? It just comes with you. We have found school holidays are the worst. At least during term time we had the boys at home with us, and the busy regular routines of school and work life kept us all busy, and connected. Take that away and we found ourselves frequently alone, sometimes for days on end in the summer months when the boys were away staying with friends or on sports camps, giving us too much time to think. Those first New Year and summer holidays were long and torturous.

Exercise: Make a plan for dealing with tiredness

Which of the following are manageable for you? Which will help you get the rest you need? Identify the times and places that fit in with your own routines and commitments.

- Sleep when you can (a 20-minute sleep is really effective).
- Find yourself a quiet space (car, a quiet corner of the office, bed, sofa), drink a decent coffee and then settle down for 20 minutes' sleep; the coffee will wake you up without needing an alarm, by which time you've had the benefit of sleep and

the coffee to keep you going. Obviously I'm not advocating drinking too much coffee, but if you simply cannot get away, this is an effective fix.

- Watch your weekday bed times—try not to add to the tiredness by forgetting to go to bed at a sensible hour.
- Watch out for the weekends. Once we'd realised that two late nights over the weekend stuffed up the whole of the next week, making everything harder and us much more miserable, we tried to be really disciplined about this.

Get out and get moving

I've long been motivated to exercise for my mental health more than for my physical health. I know how cranky I am if I don't get outside and move each day and I know, from the research and the empirical studies I've conducted, that exercise is the key to living a long and healthy life. I often quote Tal Ben-Shahar, former lecturer at Harvard and author of several books,[1] who says that not exercising is akin to taking a depressant. That is, if you're not exercising you may as well be taking a pill that makes you depressed—that's how much difference not moving makes to our lives. The research is incontrovertible: exercise *is* medicine.[2]

'Physical exercise contributes a great deal to happiness; in fact, there is research showing that regular exercise, three times a week for 30 to 40 minutes of aerobic exercise—could be jogging or walking or aerobics or dancing . . . is equivalent to some of our most powerful psychiatric drugs in dealing with depression or sadness or anxiety. We've become a sedentary culture where we park our car next to our workplace or take the train and we don't walk like our foreparents used to. Thousands of years ago our foreparents walked an average of eight miles a day. How far do we walk today? Well, it depends on where we park our car. And we pay a high price for it because we weren't made to be sedentary. We were made to be physically active.'[3]

After Abi died, and with Ben-Shahar's words foremost in my mind, I knew that moving daily was more critical than ever. But, I was also fortunate enough to have studied exercise psychology, which is an entire field dedicated to the science of making exercise happen. That's right: while sport psychologists focus on how to make professional athletes be faster, quicker and stronger, exercise psychologists are chiefly concerned with how to get the rest of us off the couch and moving a bit more often.

I knew from exercise psychology that humans are designed to live outdoors in nearly perpetual motion. As Stephen Ilardi writes in his great book *The Depression Cure*, 'human beings were never designed for the poorly nourished, sedentary, indoor, sleep-deprived, socially isolated, frenzied pace of twenty-first-century life'.[4]

Mechanisation has effectively removed the requirement for daily movement from our lives: we push buttons and flick switches to transport us from A to B, to wash our clothes, vacuum our floors, knead our bread, roast our food and even to switch TV channels. All of our clever inventions have engineered movement right out of our lives, so that our average energy expenditure per unit of body mass is now less than 38 per cent of that of our Stone Age ancestors.[5] While Paleolithic man walked five to ten miles on an average day just to find food and water, very little in our 21st-century lives requires us to physically move, push or pull, hunt or gather. As a consequence of this, we are struggling mentally and physically and, just to make it harder still, physical activity has become something of a choice. We have to opt in rather than opt out. For most of us, opting in is hard work; it's just not the obvious choice, particularly when we are grieving. But when we are stressed, we need to get out and get moving more than ever. Regular physical activity really is a magic bullet for mental health.

I'm not talking about running marathons—the type of physical activity that I'm talking about won't require you to don Lycra or join a gym. Just to get outside and move, for half an hour a day, in three ten-minute blocks is good. The research is undeniable: aerobic exercise physically transforms our brains and engaging in physical activity is the natural way to prevent the negative consequences of stress. What's more, while the evidence is relatively new, the psychological benefits of exposure to sunlight are also starting to emerge. Ilardi is big on green exercise: 'Although simply going outside on a sunny day can brighten your mood, an even deeper link exists between light exposure and depression—one involving the body's internal clock. As it turns out, the brain gauges the amount of light you get each day, and it uses that information to reset your body clock. Without enough light exposure, the body clock eventually gets out of sync, and when that happens, it throws off important circadian rhythms that regulate energy, sleep, appetite, and hormonal levels. The disruption of these important biological rhythms can, in turn, trigger clinical depression. Because natural sunlight is so much brighter than indoor lighting—over a hundred times brighter, on average—a half hour of sunlight is enough to reset your body clock. Even the natural light of a grey, cloudy day is several times brighter than the inside of most people's houses, and a few hours of exposure provide just enough light to keep circadian rhythms well regulated. But people who are inside from dawn to dusk often find their body clocks starting to malfunction.'[6]

But given that exercise is a choice, I'll be the first to acknowledge that it's not always the easiest one to make. People who don't know me well suppose that I love exercise. In some ways I do, but I also firmly, utterly loathe it too. I hate the moment the alarm goes off to tell me it's time to get up in the dark; I am full of self-pity as I go to bed and set that alarm; I'm often cross as I lace up my shoes; and if, for some glorious reason, I cannot locate my car keys in the morning, I'm only too happy to call the whole thing off and go back to bed.

REGULAR PHYSICAL ACTIVITY REALLY IS A MAGIC BULLET FOR MENTAL HEALTH.

These, according to exercise psychology, are my 'barriers' to exercise. Others are: I just can't be bothered; I hate running, I'd rather have an extra hour in bed; I'm not fit enough to keep up with the others I run with; it's raining/cold/dark/too hot; I'm too hung-over; or, currently, I'm just too plain weary with grief. Yes, there are multiple barriers to exercise.

Just as there are barriers to exercise, there is also what is known as 'enablers' to exercise—the things that motivate and enable us to get out the door. Running, for instance, is cheap (costs nothing aside from a new pair of shoes each year), it's efficient (all you need is half an hour to accrue a long list of positive physical and mental health benefits), it's social (the friends I run with can very often become the only friends I get to spend time with each day). In my case, it also involves being outdoors. Best of all? All of the above apply to walking too. It's cheap, efficient, social and, ideally, outdoors.

Walking is my favourite exercise; it ticks so many boxes. Mostly I go with Trevor and Jack The Dog, but there are times when our circle of grief, the two of us, feels too small and claustrophobic, and I instinctively know we need the support and energy of others. That's when I'll text or call a friend, knowing we need company. There are other times, though, when I relish walking alone; it gives me the opportunity to think, to cry, and reflect on what's happened, what I'm feeling and how I'm coping. I use it as an opportunity to check in with myself.

If developing a regular exercise routine has been hard for you in the past, identifying your enablers to exercise is vital. Knowing your barriers, and finding solutions to them, or the enablers that outweigh them, is equally important. Consider what your personal barriers and enablers might be by answering the questions in the exercise below.

Embarking on an exercise routine when you are grieving might seem initially like adding to your burden, not helping. But remember I'm talking only about three bouts of ten-minute walking each day. Social support is also likely to be key when you're starting out. As Stephen Ilardi writes: 'The depressed brain actually has an impaired ability to initiate activities, so those battling depression usually have a difficult time starting anything new. But they typically do just fine with a new activity if someone else can help them get going.'[7] My friend Kate helped me get back into swimming. By driving me to the pool, understanding that there are days when I might only manage ten lengths, and turning it into an enjoyable activity rather than a chore, she made this activity possible for me once or twice a week. I would never have kept it up without her.

If developing and sticking to a habit of daily physical activity has been a challenge for you, James Prochaska's change model may help you understand why you've previously fallen off the wagon and what you can do to stay on it. Prochaska and his colleagues identified that in order to develop a habit of any kind, people have to travel through five steps from 1) *precontemplation* (when we have no intention to change but the inkling of a thought is recognised) to 2) actual *contemplation* (when we first seriously consider changing a habit) to 3) progressing through *preparation* (when we consider the difficulties involved and perhaps crystallise goals) to 4) *action* (when the new behaviour begins) and finally to 5) *maintenance* (which involves us working out relapse-prevention strategies).[8]

SOCIAL SUPPORT IS LIKELY TO BE KEY WHEN YOU'RE STARTING OUT.

Their research also revealed two key pieces of evidence informing the successful adoption of an ongoing and ingrained habit of physical activity: first, that our readiness for making that habit occur is the vital indicator of success (that is, no one can be convinced to become a routine exerciser while they are still in the precontemplation stage); and, secondly, that before we can truly adopt a new habit and make it a permanent feature in our lives (i.e. reach the maintenance stage of the model) many of us have to pass through some of these stages many times. But—and here's the promising bit—each time we do so, we learn more about what successful change looks like for us individually. 'Most self-changers will recycle several times through the stages before achieving long-term maintenance,' says Prochaska,[9] explaining that the development of a fully ingrained, sustainable new habit does not happen in one steady linear progression. His model resembles an upward spiral like a corkscrew. It is well worth spending some time considering which stage of Prochaska's model you currently sit at, and what it would take for you to move through to the next stage.

Exercises for boosting daily physical activity

In the professional development workshops I run, aimed at helping employees become more resilient, I use an eight-pronged strategy for boosting daily physical activity:

1. Work out what motivates you to move more by asking yourself the following questions:
   - *Who do I want to do this for?*
   - *What difference will it make?*
   - *Why do I/they care?*
   - *How will I feel if I do manage to move more?*
   - *What is the consequence of not moving more?*

2. Plan each week. This involves working out in advance the 4Ws of activity:
   - *Who are you going to exercise with this week?*
   - *When are you going to do that?*
   - *What activities are you actually willing to commit to?*
   - *Where will this happen?*

3. Don't be put off by the word 'exercise'. If it helps, stop thinking about exercise and focus on just moving more often.

4. Be flexible: there will be days when your greatest intentions are thwarted, and days when you just can't bring yourself to get out of bed. What small thing can you do on those days to keep the habit alive?
   - *Walk to a local coffee shop mid-morning instead of driving.*
   - *Ask a friend to join you walking their/your dog.*
   - *Climb the stairs at work instead of taking the lift (when you've done it once, you're more likely to repeat that success).*
   - *Park as far away from the supermarket as you can, then walk.*
   - *Get the bus instead of driving to work.*

5. Be kind to yourself: grief is exhausting and not the time to set yourself strenuous and unrealistic exercise goals. Do what you can: something is better than nothing, every time.

6. Sign up for an event to increase your motivation: find something that appeals to you and is manageable (perhaps a sponsored walk or cycle).

7. Buy a dog! I've long considered dogs one of the best wellbeing promoters there is: offering love, requiring walks, making us laugh, our dog has been such a compassionate friend and a fantastic antidote to grief.

8. Use a Fitbit to monitor your daily activity patterns. Using goalsetting and feedback software is a great way to boost motivation.

FUSING PHYSICAL ACTIVITY WITH SOCIAL CONNECTION

Dr Elaine O'Brien has for more than 20 years run her FitDance movement class based around her academic research into the importance of social fitness. Based on the principles of Positive Enjoyable Exercises Promoting Strengths (PEEPS), she has built and sustained a thriving community of exercisers aged 71–81 years old. When I first met Elaine, I imagined how much this vital, energetic woman must give to her group of aging movers and shakers. But, digging deeper for this book, I realised just how much of a win–win this class has been for her too as she watched her father die and tackled her bereavement.

'That class has helped give my life meaning, purpose and has sustained me during my lowest times of bereavement and grief,' she explains. Based on the 'moai' (an Okinawan practice whereby a group of good friends support each other, share life's fortunes and woes, and meet for a common purpose), FitDance is aimed at helping increase cardiovascular health, strength, balance, flexibility and core development. But, just as importantly, the social fitness underpinnings are expressly aimed at building and promoting kinship, camaraderie and support among attendees. 'The moai is a safe place to laugh, cry, gain strength and give support. The moai in our FitDance programme offers an opportunity to confer, care and create a sense of purpose for each member of the group,' explained Dr O'Brien.

'Many of the wonderful women in my dance/fitness programme have been widowed, some for many years. These vibrant, active older women have meaningful lives that connect them to the larger world. I fully recognise that the relationships we have with others, our environment and our selves are a truly important part of the bereavement process. The women in my classes know that I love and care about them. Each . . . has been there for me, and has helped me through some of the darkest hours of my life. Many group members have been participating in the FitDance programme for from 5 to 15 years, and new members are always heartily welcomed into this whole fitness training. It has evolved into a loving, social support network.'

Dr O'Brien is passionate in spreading the word about the importance of PEEPS—physical activity as a positive strategy for life, making it enjoyable so that her participants want to return—and for building therapeutic relationships, and thriving individuals, workplaces and communities. 'Being strong in mind, body and spirit offers a beautiful framework for resilience, helping lift us up, and cope through tragedy, bereavement and grief,' she concludes.

She also has these tips for people struggling to start and maintain a regular routine of being physically active:

- Ideally, exercise should have a fun factor to keep up the enjoyment, offer some challenge and encouragement, leaving participants wanting more. Making exercise play, and fun, will increase the possibility that you will continue on with building an enjoyable exercise habit.
- Practise self-care and self-compassion. Get rest, exercise, eat well, go out and breathe in fresh air, and take care of yourself. We need to care for ourselves, and then for others. Think

of the law of the oxygen mask on an airplane—fit your own mask first, then attend to your children.

- One of the best ways to sabotage an exercise habit is to start too fast or hard. Ideally, new and experienced exercisers need to listen to their bodies, take it at a comfortable yet challenging pace, be given appropriate movement modifications, build progression each time, apply a variety of forms of movement and consider balanced movement, of varying intensities (again building progression), for different time durations, at frequent intervals during the day.

- Make a date to walk, even better if it is with friends. When you walk, mix it up. Start with an easy warm-up, giving you and your friends time to visit, and after a set time period (five minutes), pick up the pace. You can start with even five seconds of higher-intensity walking—a faster, longer stride, with focus on posture and alignment. After higher-intensity walking for a bit, go back to a more moderate pace. Changing the movement packs a powerful punch, lifting up physical, cognitive and emotional benefits.

- Think of the activities you enjoyed as a child and see how those might be modified for you to enjoy right now.

- Remember that physical activity is at least as relevant to the mind as it is to the body—that might just motivate you more![10]

REAPPRAISAL
AND
RENEWAL

Chapter 13

Reappraising your brave new world

IT IS WIDELY ACKNOWLEDGED among bereavement researchers that the death of a loved one frequently induces a crisis of meaning—and that being able to decipher the personal impact of the loss and construct some kind of new life narrative is an integral part of that adjustment.[1] 'Bereavement is a powerful experience, even for the most resilient among us, and it sometimes dramatically shifts our perspective on life. Under normal circumstances, most of us cruise through our busy days without the slightest thought of life and death . . . The death of a loved one tends to peel back the curtain on those existential questions, at least temporarily, and begs us to take a larger view of the world and our place in it,' explains George Bonanno.[2]

The death of someone we love rocks our world, literally, throwing us off our expected path, shattering our sense of safety and personal security, and prompting some hefty personal questioning on, well, pretty much *everything*—from am I in the right job, living in the right place and with the right partner, to what's the point in life if it just ends in death? How do I go on living a normal existence, knowing that such terrible things can happen and that everyone I love will inevitably die? How can I trust that this won't happen again? What is the purpose and meaning of life?

Death provides us with a painfully stark reminder that life has no guarantees and we can't necessarily count on tomorrow. Bereavement, in short, induces a period of reappraisal. Thomas Attig writes beautifully about this, describing how bereavement uproots our souls and shakes our spirits. How, ultimately, it is a process of *relearning the world*. 'We do eventually have to find the courage, faith, and hope we need to reengage in the world, take tentative first steps, try fail, try again, fail better, and eventually relearn how to be and act in the world that loss changed so profoundly.'[3] He continues: 'The next chapters cannot unfold just as we expected, hoped, or dreamed they would'; life's coherence and meaning are shattered. Welcome to your new world.

It took me a while to understand this after Abi's death, and my new mantra became to 'trust the process'—to trust that this new normal will eventually become bearable and that there will one day be hope, meaning, purpose and love in this new unchartered land. I know Abi's loss has fundamentally changed me—a stark line now runs through my life, dividing the time before and after Abi's death. The old me and the new me.

One of the biggest tasks is to re-establish our world order, somehow aligning what's happened with our overall life story.

My sister-in-law's mother wrote to me in that first week after Abi's death to share useful words of advice she'd been offered when her husband died suddenly a few years back: 'You will never get over it, it's never going to be okay, and once you accept that, you realise that you would never want to get over it. Just kind of let it sit with you, and let it be part of who you are.'

For us, this required us learning to imagine a fulfilled future without Abi in it. As parents we constantly project forward to what the years ahead may bring for our children. Over time we have grown accustomed to nurturing their hopes and dreams and, consciously or not, we'd developed the whisper of a potential prototype of the adult Abi's life. She'd given us the clues, and we'd built her future self around that scaffolding. In just one term at her new middle/high school she'd become part of the Future Problem Solvers and debating teams. Marching through the front door after school one day, she'd asked, 'Mum, is it possible to be too solution focused?' I laughed with glee at the twelve-year-old familiar with the concept of being solution focused. She was always quizzing me about my work and daily scribbled slightly mad-capped entries into her gratitude diary at school. 'We'll publish together one day,' I told her. 'Hone & Hone, 2030.'

So what happens to these unrequited thoughts and futile dreams once the protagonist has gone? You can't just turn them off. What happens is that we are forced, over time, to rewrite the future, to devise a new life scheme. I know I'll never watch a blonde carefree girl dancing in a bikini without thinking of her, or visit New York without imagining the life she'd dreamed of there (or Spain or Italy—on the upside, she's never going to marry any of those Italian men Trevor used to have nightmares about). Right now, I still like to imagine the 21st party we'll have in her honour—with family and her friends gathered, tears and songs to take us back and celebrate her short life. We'll dream of what might have been, acknowledging what we collectively lost. But I know that my future imaginings now must focus on four, not five, of us. I'm rewriting the future.

Developing a sense of meaning around what has happened and working it into a new version of your life story is an important part of successfully adapting to grief. Research has shown two different types of meaning to be especially relevant to the grief context. They are meaning in the form of *sense-making* and in the sense of *benefit-finding*.

> DEVELOPING A SENSE OF MEANING
> AROUND WHAT HAS HAPPENED AND
> WORKING IT INTO A NEW VERSION OF
> YOUR LIFE STORY IS AN IMPORTANT PART
> OF SUCCESSFULLY ADAPTING TO GRIEF.

Sense-making involves the bereaved successfully placing the death into our own world view, so that it makes sense. Examples might include understanding that a smoker died of lung cancer, or that God took a loved one into his care, or, in our case, that death doesn't discriminate and that accidents can happen to anyone at any time.

Benefit-finding occurs when we derive meaning from the loss by acknowledging positive consequences (a new appreciation for the preciousness of life, greater perspective, improved relationships, and augmented empathy and compassion for others).[4] In the course of writing this book, I corresponded with a woman who had suffered a series of traumatic events, including two children requiring years of surgeries and the loss of a child in utero. In our discussions of grief, Alicia Assad was concerned that she had not suffered the death of a loved one in the same way as many readers will have. But her experiences with her children over those tumultuous years certainly confronted her with loss, and the way layer upon layer of trauma forced her to reappraise her life has lessons for the bereaved. Her experiences prompted her own research on recovery and trauma, culminating in a website featuring many of the tools mentioned in this book (optimism, mindfulness, hope and relationships): see www.beautifulcrisis.com.

'My initial hope was that my family would reach a time free from adversity. Yet after repeated traumatic events, I experienced a disruption of my core beliefs. I had to make a choice between losing hope and redefining what hope meant to me,' she wrote. She chose the latter. 'According to Snyder's Hope Theory, hope is supported by having a realistic goal, multiple pathways to reach it, and a sense of agency, that is, a belief that I can follow the pathways. So I redefined hope by first selecting a more realistic goal: "I hope that tomorrow I find the strength to endure whatever I have to face." Then I clearly defined multiple pathways to reach my new goal: "If something bad happens again, I will lean on my friends and family for strength." My sense of agency came from remembering what I had already managed to endure, and appreciating my strengthened resilience.'

Redefining hope, though, was only one step in the process of healing for Alicia. 'I still needed to grapple with my aching desire to right what was wrong, especially given the pain my son had endured. I wished to erase every horrible experience from my past. Given this was as unrealistic as my initial hope goal, I needed to accept what happened to my family and develop a more productive explanation. For example, I could look at my son as a burn victim who is badly scarred and negatively affected by his injury, or I could see him as a survivor who had exemplified more strength and courage than I knew a small boy was capable of. When I see him as a survivor, every scar is symbolic of his bravery. I can choose to see the beauty in my son's physical scars as well as my own emotional scars.' This is benefit-finding at work: Alicia is rewriting the narrative of her experiences, seeking any positives to come from the misery. She has what she refers to as a 'suppressed appreciation for the good that can come from our most difficult experiences'. She does not welcome trauma, but its presence in her life has prompted her to evolve a new philosophy on hope—one that allows her to move forward without being crippled by fear. 'I don't believe that my son's accident happened for a reason. I don't believe I lost that baby for a reason. But to heal I have needed to look back and find the good that has come from these hard experiences. At least in my case, that is how I have been able to move forward. Even in the darkest moments there were blessings. I had to choose to notice they were there.'[5]

This process of reappraisal, the search for the meaning of the loss, and a re-jigging of our sense of the future to incorporate the event into our own personal narrative, is now acknowledged as a key process of grieving. Knowing this is at the core of my own motivation for writing this book: faced with Abi's loss, I hoped it might make some sense out of the senseless.

BENEFIT-FINDING, AKA 'ACCEPT THE GOOD'

For all the additional trauma that comes from a sudden death, it does have its benefits, I told myself. Abi died suddenly. We didn't have to watch her suffer, give up hope; she was at least spared that agony. Instead the agony is ours alone. There is some good in that.

This kind of reframing (benefit-finding) is our brain's natural way of helping us cope. It involves shifting our perspective, choosing what we focus on. It is different from absolute denial of what has happened; we know that it has happened, our brains are just searching for different outlooks and interpretations of aspects of her death to keep the helplessness at bay. Benefit-finding is recognised as a highly effective coping strategy. If you want to cope, find something to be pleased about. Resilient people manage to think about traumatic events flexibly, so that, when the worst happens, they manage to re-evaluate what's happened and put a different spin on it—along the lines of 'what doesn't kill you makes you stronger'. This is not to say that people exposed to trauma are grateful for the opportunity to change as a result of adverse events, just that they are good at reframing it, assimilating the experience into part of their identity, and can accept it and recover.

'Accept the good' has become something of a mantra for Trevor and me. Our good friend Charlie lent us a fluoro pink poster when she was leaving the country to visit her sister-in-law who was undergoing chemotherapy—it serves to remind us to appreciate the good things that can so easily go unnoticed in a sea of misery.

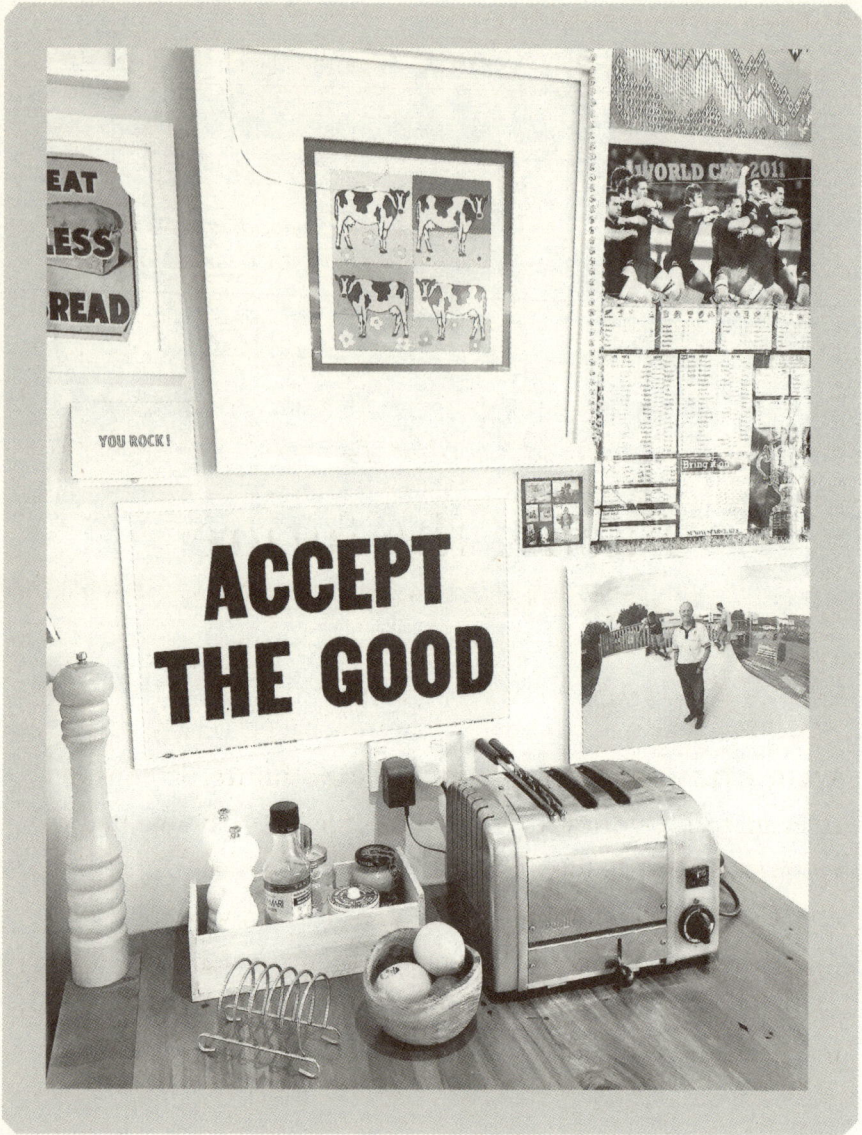

Chapter 14

Facing the future

THIS CHAPTER IS FOCUSED on the future. It considers strategies and stories from other people that have helped me venture cautiously forward without Abi's physical presence by my side, but knowing she is safely stowed in my heart.

Below are three stories that represent tiny pieces in my jigsaw of recovery. They are stories that provided me with ideas and inspiration to spur me on.

Option B: Sheryl Sandberg

Sheryl Sandberg, COO of Facebook, lost her husband, Dave Goldberg, in May 2015, and described the impact of his loss in a Facebook post that resonated with me.

Today is the end of sheloshim for my beloved husband—the first thirty days. Judaism calls for a period of intense mourning known as shiva that lasts seven days after a loved one is buried. After shiva, most normal activities can be resumed, but it is the end of sheloshim that marks the completion of religious mourning for a spouse.

A childhood friend of mine who is now a rabbi recently told me that the most powerful one-line prayer he has ever read is: 'Let me not die while I am still alive.' I would have never understood that prayer before losing Dave. Now I do.

I think when tragedy occurs, it presents a choice. You can give in to the void, the emptiness that fills your heart, your lungs, constricts your ability to think or even breathe. Or you can try to find meaning. These past thirty days, I have spent many of my moments lost in that void. And I know that many future moments will be consumed by the vast emptiness as well.

But when I can, I want to choose life and meaning.

And this is why I am writing: to mark the end of sheloshim and to give back some of what others have given to me. While the experience of grief is profoundly personal, the bravery of those who have shared their own experiences has helped pull me through. Some who opened their hearts were my closest friends. Others were total strangers who have shared wisdom and advice publicly. So I am sharing what I have learned in the hope that it helps someone else. In the hope that there can be some meaning from this tragedy.

I have lived thirty years in these thirty days. I am thirty years sadder. I feel like I am thirty years wiser.

I have gained a more profound understanding of what it is to be a mother, both through the depth of the agony I feel when my children scream and cry and from the connection my mother has to my pain. She has tried to fill the empty space in my bed, holding me each night until I cry myself to sleep. She has fought to hold back her own tears to make room for mine. She has explained to me that the anguish I am feeling is both my own and my children's, and I understood that she was right as I saw the pain in her own eyes.

I have learned that I never really knew what to say to others in need. I think I got this all wrong before; I tried to assure people that it would be okay, thinking that hope was the most comforting thing I could offer. A friend of mine with late-stage cancer told me that the worst thing people could say to him was 'It is going to be okay.' That voice in his head would scream, How do you know it is going to be okay? Do you not understand that I might die? I learned this past month what he was trying to teach me. Real empathy is sometimes not insisting that it will be okay but acknowledging that it is not. When people say to me, 'You and your children will find happiness again,' my heart tells me, Yes, I believe that, but I know I will never feel pure joy again. Those who have said, 'You will find a new normal, but it will never be as good' comfort me more because they know and speak the truth. Even a simple 'How are you?'—almost always asked with the best of intentions—is better replaced with 'How are you today?' When I am asked 'How are you?' I stop myself from shouting, My husband died a month ago, how do you think I am? When I hear 'How are you today?' I realise the person knows that the best I can do right now is to get through each day.

I have learned some practical stuff that matters. Although we now know that Dave died immediately, I didn't know that in the ambulance. The trip to the hospital was unbearably slow. I still hate every car that did not move to the side, every person who cared more about arriving at their destination a few minutes earlier than making room for us to pass. I have noticed this while driving in many countries and

185

cities. Let's all move out of the way. Someone's parent or partner or child might depend on it.

I have learned how ephemeral everything can feel—and maybe everything is. That whatever rug you are standing on can be pulled right out from under you with absolutely no warning. In the last thirty days, I have heard from too many women who lost a spouse and then had multiple rugs pulled out from under them. Some lack support networks and struggle alone as they face emotional distress and financial insecurity. It seems so wrong to me that we abandon these women and their families when they are in greatest need.

I have learned to ask for help—and I have learned how much help I need. Until now, I have been the older sister, the COO [Chief Operating Officer], the doer and the planner. I did not plan this, and when it happened, I was not capable of doing much of anything. Those closest to me took over. They planned. They arranged. They told me where to sit and reminded me to eat. They are still doing so much to support me and my children.

I have learned that resilience can be learned. Adam M. Grant taught me that three things are critical to resilience and that I can work on all three. Personalisation—realising it is not my fault. He told me to ban the word 'sorry'. To tell myself over and over, This is not my fault. Permanence—remembering that I won't feel like this forever. This will get better. Pervasiveness—this does not have to affect every area of my life; the ability to compartmentalise is healthy.

For me, starting the transition back to work has been a saviour, a chance to feel useful and connected. But I quickly discovered that even those connections had changed. Many of my co-workers had a look of fear in their eyes as I approached. I knew why—they wanted to help but weren't sure how. Should I mention it? Should I not mention it? If I mention it, what the hell do I say? I realised that to restore that closeness with my colleagues that has always been so important to me, I needed to let them in. And that meant being more open and vulnerable than I ever wanted to be. I told those I work with most closely that they could ask me their honest questions and I would answer. I also said it was okay for them to talk about how they felt. One colleague admitted she'd been driving by my house frequently, not sure if she should come in. Another said he was paralysed when I was around, worried he might say the wrong thing. Speaking openly replaced the fear of doing and saying the wrong thing. One of my favourite cartoons of all time has an elephant in a room answering the phone, saying, 'It's the elephant.' Once I addressed the elephant, we were able to kick him out of the room.

At the same time, there are moments when I can't let people in. I went to Portfolio Night at school where kids show their parents around the classroom to look at their work hung on the walls. So many of the parents—all of whom have been so kind—tried to make eye contact or say something they thought would be comforting. I looked down the entire time so no one could catch my eye for fear of breaking down. I hope they understood.

I have learned gratitude. Real gratitude for the things I took for granted before—like life. As heartbroken as I am, I look at my children each day and rejoice that they are alive. I appreciate every smile, every hug. I no longer take each day for granted. When a friend told me that he hates birthdays and so he was not celebrating his, I looked at him and said through tears, 'Celebrate your birthday, goddammit. You are lucky to have each one.' My next birthday will be depressing as hell, but I am determined to celebrate it in my heart more than I have ever celebrated a birthday before.

I am truly grateful to the many who have offered their sympathy. A colleague told me that his wife, whom I have never met, decided to show her support by going back to school to get her degree—something she had been putting off for years. Yes! When the circumstances allow, I believe as much as ever in leaning in. And so many men—from those I know well to those I will likely never know—are honouring Dave's life by spending more time with their families.

I can't even express the gratitude I feel to my family and friends who have done so much and reassured me that they will continue to be there. In the brutal moments when I am overtaken by the void, when the months and years stretch out in front of me endless and empty, only their faces pull me out of the isolation and fear. My appreciation for them knows no bounds.

I was talking to one of these friends about a father–child activity that Dave is not here to do. We came up with a plan to fill in for Dave. I cried to him, 'But I want Dave. I want option A.' He put his arm around me and said, 'Option A is not available. So let's just kick the shit out of option B.'

Dave, to honour your memory and raise your children as they deserve to be raised, I promise to do all I can to kick the shit out of option B.[1]

Kicking the shit out of option B has become a mantra for me. Just the other day I found myself in bed, silently sobbing, thinking, It's not okay, it's just not okay, I don't want to have to live this way. But when option A is no longer possible, then, yes, I too will commit to kicking the shit out of option B. Thank you, Sheryl.

Having a survivor mission: Marcie Warrington and Joe Kasper

People who survive trauma and go on to thrive very often have what Charney and Southwick refer to as a 'survivor mission'—a mission to help others, to make something good come from the misery they've been forced to endure. In my own research and interviews with people who have displayed remarkable resilience in the face of grief, the power of altruism, or a survivor mission, to propel growth often shines through. For example, in November 2014 the people I work with at the Values in Action Institute in Cincinnati introduced me to Marcie Warrington. Her mission to help herself and others to 'live well' has fuelled her recovery and transformation following her 17-year-old son Johnny's violent death.

For many years, as it is for so many grieving mothers, I wasn't sure I'd survive his loss. Then one day, nearly four years on, I realised I had survived, and would likely continue to survive. The question of life, not just survival, now loomed large before me. At that time I realised the future could so easily become nothing more than an endurance contest, one I could win, as the past four years had shown. But living well requires much more than that. My love for my son and his love for me deserves more than endurance. It calls for, even demands, living well. I now realise that our love is so much bigger than mere survival, endurance contests, even death. Living with this eternal love, each day, was the answer for me, and the direction for my future.

Love is infinite, not limited to a specific recipient. While we can never replace our children (nor would we ever want to), we can honour them, their life, and the love we share. We can wake up and dedicate each day to the love of our child and make our focus the spreading of that love to others both near and far.[2]

For Marcie Warrington, the realisation that her new life mission was to assist bereaved mothers was the impetus behind her organisation, MotherLOVE (www.motherlove.net). Designed to support bereaved mothers after the death of a child, to rebuild their capacity to give and receive love, MotherLOVE offers a variety of evidence-based programmes helping mothers to live a meaningful and fulfilling life: workshops and weekend retreats; volunteer opportunities across the USA, and working with partner organisations in Tanzania and Ethiopia; plus the MotherLOVE website providing comprehensive resources, support and mentoring for bereaved mothers.

'It is important to note that living well does not necessarily mean we ever completely stop grieving. I miss my boy every day. Living well means accepting all that life has to offer us, all the pain, the joy; both sides of love's coin. But I can vouch for the long lasting benefit that comes from living and loving among HIV+ and extreme poverty in a strange country—it puts things in perspective. It is like being turned on your head,' she continues.

A colleague of mine, Joe Kasper, who lost his teenage son Ryan to Lafora's disease in 2011, refers to this kind of grief response as 'co-destiny'—when the bereaved take on a new role in life as a direct result of the loss of their loved one.

In Ryan's eulogy, Kasper described the impact of Ryan's life on his own, and how Ryan would continue to influence his actions even after his death. 'Ryan through his life; through his disease; and through his death has taught me so much about the meaning of life. I have reaped a bounty of lessons on character, handling adversity, overcoming fear and fulfilling one's purpose in life. In short, he has made me the man I am and will be the main influence on the man I will become. My student has become my teacher. Ryan, you have fulfilled your destiny.'[3] Looking back on what he'd written, Kasper explained later, he recognised these words as demonstrating his intention to incorporate the lessons of Ryan's life into his own worldview, 'thus forming a new destiny for myself that incorporates much of his personality and, in doing so, forming a co-destiny with my son'. Their relationship hadn't ended with Ryan's death.

'For the weeks following Ryan's death I continued to write about the importance of fulfilling one's destiny and stumbled upon the concept of a co-destiny. It was at that time I knew what I had to do. I realised that my destiny was to live my life in a way that would make my son proud. I knew to accomplish this I was to help others who had suffered the loss of their child to not only survive the ordeal of their child's death, but to grow from it. The awareness that I could add "goodness" to my son's life by doing "good" in his name motivates me to this day,' he explains.

When I first encountered Kasper's thoughts on co-destiny it took a while for it to sink in, but now I realise that writing this book is in many ways my expression of co-destiny with Abi, just as MotherLOVE is for Marcie Warrington, or Mothers Against Drunk Driving (MADD) is for Candace Lightner and Cindi Lamb, and the Modern Widows Club is for Carolyn Moor. These actions we have taken to honour, and in many ways in partnership with, the loved ones we lost, allow their legacies to live on in us.

What's your Giveaway? Rachel Remen

Dr Rachel Remen is clinical professor of Family and Community Medicine at UCSF School of Medicine, and founder and director of the Institute for the Study of Health and Illness at Commonweal in Ohio. As a medical educator, therapist and teacher, she has encouraged thousands of physicians to practise medicine from the heart, and thousands of patients to remember their power to heal.

Belief in the 'Giveaway' can be traced back to the North American Indian nations of the high plains. Our personal, sacred Giveaway is what we alone have come to contribute to life, our reason for being. Knowing and honouring your Giveaway imbues life with a sense of meaning and belonging, a sense of direction.

Everything is born knowing its Giveaway: trees and birds, stars and flowers know their Giveaway. Nothing is here at random. Everything belongs. Only humans are born not knowing their Giveaway, not remembering why they are here and how they belong.

From earliest infancy the Giveaway of each child can be seen and discerned by others. Helping every child recognise its unique Giveaway, its unique place of belonging is one of the most important functions of The Elders and the tribe. They observe the baby with stillness and patience. They look for signs with caring and watchful eyes. What is the baby drawn to? What draws its interest, what calms it? What makes it laugh with joy and what causes it sorrow or pain? What gifts come easily to it, what qualities are natural to it? They dream dreams for the baby that offer insight about the baby's nature and its Giveaway. There is much help to come home to yourself.

No one says 'good job' to such a child, no one influences the recognition that can only come from within by their approval and praise or their disapproval and criticism. Everyone helps the child to listen. The Giveaway of each child is a shared discovery, different for every child, every man and every woman. All Giveaways matter.

Our western experience is, of course, quite different. I recently went to visit a young friend and meet her 3-month-old son. When I arrived I found the baby sitting in a cloth jumper seat on the kitchen table watching 'BABY EINSTEIN' on a laptop. Around him on the table were many brightly coloured and noisy toys. As we talked and had a cup of tea together the young mother presented her son with toy after toy, taking one away and offering him another every few minutes. At my questioning look she laughed 'It's the newest theory,' she told me. 'The forming brain is highly plastic and needs constant stimulation.' By the time our tea was over I had learned that the baby was already registered for a prestigious private high school, Class of 2029, and letters had been written in his behalf to Princeton by his grandfathers both alumni of that institution. Other august Princeton graduates had been asked to write letters as well, the young mother told me. Chances looked good. I looked at this little boy wondering why he had come. Hoping he might someday be able to discover his Giveaway despite the powerful messages he would be given about who he was and how he was to be from the very beginning.

The closer we are able to live to our own unique Giveaway the stronger and more resilient we are despite external pressures, the more passionately and joyfully we can live, the deeper the satisfaction we feel in our daily lives and the greater the difference we can make in the world.

These ideas hold a certain magnetism for me now. What if you could find and follow your Giveaway at any age? And what if you could find your tribe, the people who watch and listen and help you to give birth to yourself? What if you already knew many such people but had not recognised why you were drawn to them? What if you could help others in this way as well? What if you did not need some catastrophic event like an illness or the loss of a loved one to finally remember who you are and why you are here?[4]

All three of these stories resonate with me because they draw us back to life, encouraging us to take on board the lessons that bereavement has taught us, and to identify how they've shaped and altered our future direction. The worst thing about death is that it is so final, permanent and unchangeable. And yet, the pause it brings to our lives, the reflection and introspection we are forced to endure, also provide the opportunity for reconsideration and, sometimes, the impetus for change.

Chapter 15

Continuing the bond

GRIEF IS A BY-PRODUCT of love. Because we loved, so must we grieve when the person we love is no longer physically with us. But the fact that they've gone doesn't mean that we must stop loving them, or thinking about them. Coming to terms with this fact, understanding that your love for that person never dies, is a major advance in our understanding of grief.

In the first year after Abi's death I missed her physical presence so badly. It took all that time, and some, to get used to her just not being here any more: to grow accustomed to her not being part of our daily routines; not there to kiss goodnight or have breakfast with in the morning; no more after-school activities to drive her to, hair to comb, fantasy books to share, shops to browse, boyfriends to discuss, waves to jump, card games to play, or rom-coms to watch. The local swimming pool and netball courts were gone from the routine of our lives. The loss of her physical presence, and particularly her and her friends' constant noise, was huge.

But, as time has passed, I've been forced to get used to that, and have grown to accept it. As much as it saddens me to say it, I no longer expect her to walk in the front door, to hear her steps outside our office, to see her face at the breakfast table, to hang out her washing, to buy her shampoo or Shapes, her favourite lunchbox snacks. I have now accepted that. My brain has caught up with the harsh reality.

Yet I also know that she has not completely gone from my life. She is very much part of me, of the life I lived, the one I live now, the places I inhabit. She is much loved, well remembered and frequently talked about. Somehow, Abi Hone is still a part of our lives. She's just not here physically. She happened, she existed, she *was* very, very real. I can keep her present in myriad small ways: consciously imagining which skirt she would pick out for me for special occasions; wearing a tiny ring that reminds me of her every day; visiting places she loved; catching up with her friends; blasting out her favourite songs and, very occasionally, snuggling down in her bed to read one of her most treasured books.

George Bonanno's *The Other Side of Sadness* is packed with observations about resilient grievers, and the common habits they adopt. One chapter covers the different ways the bereaved maintain their connections with the dead, such as keeping in touch with their loved ones' friends, treasuring precious items as keepsakes, visiting places they loved, finding time for peace and quiet in their lives because that was something the deceased taught them to value, and even talking to the dead.

'Regardless of what the relationship was actually like, resilient people are generally better able to gain a feeling of comfort from remembering the relationship during bereavement. They are also more likely to find comfort in talking about or thinking about the deceased, which, they report, makes them feel happy or at peace,' explains Bonanno.[1]

Fortunately, the historical psychological view that successful grieving required us to sever our bonds with the deceased has been very much overturned. It is now commonly accepted that working out some way to continue the bond forms part of healthy adaptation. Thomas Attig is another who writes thoughtfully about this: 'We can continue to "have" what we have "lost", that is, a continuing, albeit transformed, love for the deceased. We have not truly lost our years of living with the deceased or our memories. Nor have we lost their influences, the inspirations, the values, and the meanings embodied in their lives. We can actively incorporate these into new patterns of living that include the transformed but abiding relationships with those we have cared about and loved.'[2] He has helped me understand that developing ways of continuing bonds is particularly common practice among parents grieving the loss of their child. Similarly, studies show that the practice of maintaining bonds is common among children in mourning for their parents too: one study found that two-thirds of children still felt connected with their dead parent by speaking to them, thinking of them, dreaming of them or feeling watched by them two years after their death.[3]

The final task of Worden's Four Tasks of Mourning (see Chapter 4) is to find an enduring connection with the deceased in the midst of embarking on a new life: 'To find a place for the deceased that will enable the mourner to be connected with the deceased but in a way that will not preclude him or her from going on with life,' he writes. 'We need to find ways to memorialise, that is, to remember the dead loved ones—keeping them with us but still going on with life.'4 Essentially, the aim is to keep them with you, but in a way that allows you to go on living.

FIND AN ENDURING CONNECTION WITH THE DECEASED IN THE MIDST OF EMBARKING ON A NEW LIFE.

There is much in Worden's language that resonates with me. It is a new life that we are embarking upon. It is not one I like, and certainly isn't one I would have chosen. But I can either embrace this life, the only one I've got, or not. So, for my boys, I'm working on engaging in this new life of mine, and this book is one way for me to establish an enduring connection with Abi. The dream of publishing with my girl is no longer going to happen, but I could not (would not) have written this particular book without her.

Abi is plainly visible in almost every aspect of our lives. Some of her things are still scattered around the house—her Ugg boots sit among our other shoes by the front door, her hair clips mingle with mine in the little bag we always shared, her bedroom still has her photos up, even though friends and family sleep in it all the time and we have, of course, packed away her clothes. We talk about her, share funny memories, laugh about her moods and infuriating fussy eating habits. I occasionally watch terrible TV shows just because she loved them. Her sunglasses hang among the paraphernalia in Trevor's truck, and though we've given away her wetsuit, I occasionally come across her booties in the chaos of the garage. Some of these are deliberate efforts to keep her memory alive; others have evolved for one reason or another, perhaps because it's too painful and unnecessary to find a home for her Uggs and I still enjoy rifling through her hairgrips in the morning, or just because we're busy and it requires too much energy to locate both booties and find a caring home for them. In the meantime, these things give me comfort.

I've given a great deal away, but I've also been mindful not to scatter her precious possessions too hastily. They are a finite resource after all; there will be no more. I've kept her school uniform in a wicker trunk, beautifully folded for me by my sister Esther; and I enjoy drying my wet hair in the Barbie towel she always wrapped around her head. I could have sold her school uniform or handed it out to friends, but I've kept it for now—partly because it's too small to be useful to others for long, and partly because at some point in the future I might like to make a quilt cover of her favourite clothes. In all likelihood, I won't, but confronting these things has not seemed a good use of my energy so far. And for now, they provide a degree of comfort and ongoing connection. To deny that she was such a big part of our family life and rid our home of her presence seems an illogical stance. It is still our family home, home to all three of our children, and that offers me a modicum of comfort.

My friend Denise recently told me she sometimes chooses to wear loved relatives' jewellery with a similar purpose. 'Without planning it I realise that I have developed a way of having my important people around me. I didn't like the idea of them being gone and not hearing or seeing what's going on. I have a pantheon, not of gods, but of departed people whom I miss and think of all the time. They are there, looking down and seeing what's going on. They are watching over me and available to me for support and advice. I think of them very often and so they have to be nearby,' she explains.[5] Denise prefers to think of this as 'not grieving but remembering', and describes wearing loved ones' jewellery as like putting on armour for battle. 'I feel worthy and lovable when I wear these things and also like I am participating in an ancient ritual. The idea that I am no different from some pagan ancestor thousands of years ago makes me smile and is also good for putting the day into perspective. Whatever happens in the day I know I am loved and worthwhile and connected to this sense of value and place in the world. Nothing can penetrate this armour.'

According to Bonanno, the bereaved who cope best are able to find comfort in ongoing connections. 'They know their loved one is gone, but when they think and talk about the deceased, they find that they haven't lost everything. The relationship is not completely gone. They can still call to mind and find joy in the positive shared experiences. It is as if some part of the relationship is still alive.'[6]

One of those ongoing connections came from a very unexpected source. We were fortunate to have Alex Fulton, Abi's godmother, take over the selection and decoration of her coffin for us. I could not face it. Alex, a designer, retailer and colour consultant, chose to cover the coffin in hundreds of vinyl dots in Abi's favourite colours, which, subsequently, we have sprinkled throughout our lives. They became known as 'Abi's

Dots'. Family and friends now have these brightly coloured dots on the back of their phones, on cars, laptops, bed heads, guitars, suitcases, wallets, windows, bikes, skis, helmets and so on. They are frequently displayed in a cluster of three dots to remember Abi, Ella and Sally.

THE BEREAVED WHO COPE BEST ARE ABLE TO FIND COMFORT IN ONGOING CONNECTIONS.

The dots have proved an unexpected, but powerful, legacy for our loved ones. When I'm driving around town and I see them on the back of an unfamiliar car, I realise it's other people's way of saying 'we feel your pain' and showing that our girls are not forgotten. Those small colourful dots remind us to make the most of the one life we have, and they connect us to the girls. For this reason, they've become the symbol of my website and blog *One Wild and Precious Life*, named after the Mary Oliver poem that Sally shared with me 18 months before she died. It's such a fitting poem for Sally, who was so good at noticing the beauty every day. And who fully grasped the urgency of making the most of our one wild and precious life. She was both wild and precious, and died too soon.

Almost 100,000 Abi's Dots have been sold from Alex's website and shop. On Instagram, we have witnessed them springing up in Paris, London, Croatia, New York, Singapore, Fiji, Samoa, right across America and literally from the top to the bottom of New Zealand. Donating $12 from each sale, Alex Fulton Design has so far contributed $11,500 to Starship's Make A Wish Foundation. It feels good to have made something worthwhile come from something so bad. A collaboration that arose from grief and loss has helped connect people throughout the world as they share love through colour. Abi's Dots and the myriad ways we've established to honour and remember her have helped me understand that she will always be part of our lives, despite her physical absence. She (her life, her death, everything) has a profound influence on who we are as people, how we choose to live our lives, how we choose to treat other people, and the projects we choose to dedicate time and energy to.

Exercise: 10 things they loved

My friend Gretchen described to me how several years earlier she and her husband had suddenly lost someone dear to them. 'At his funeral his brother-in-law named 10 things Tobin loved (rugby, raising a glass of cold beer, being a flight medic, kicking the soccer ball with his girls . . .) and asked that each of us remember Tobin each time one of those 10 things happen and say his name out loud. It's been close to seven years now and Mike and I still do this. What began as a grieving ritual turned into a very loving way to bring him regularly to us.' This kind of enduring acknowledgement reassures the bereaved that the deceased are still remembered.

What are the 10 things your loved one loved that will always
remind you of them?
Which clothes?
Which places?
Which particular activities?
Which sports?

Which movies?
Which songs?
Which times of the year and celebrations/holidays?
Which types of food and what were their favourite recipes?
What was their must-have item on holiday?
Which books?

. . . .

The Summer Day

Who made the world?
Who made the swan, and the black bear?
Who made the grasshopper?
This grasshopper, I mean—
the one who has flung herself out of the grass,
the one who is eating sugar out of my hand,
who is moving her jaws back and forth instead of up
      and down—
who is gazing around with her enormous and
      complicated eyes.
Now she lifts her pale forearms and thoroughly washes
      her face.
Now she snaps her wings open, and floats away.
I don't know exactly what a prayer is.
I do know how to pay attention, how to fall down
into the grass, how to kneel down in the grass,
how to be idle and blessed, how to stroll through
      the fields,
which is what I have been doing all day.
Tell me, what else should I have done?
Doesn't everything die at last, and too soon?
Tell me, what is it you plan to do
with your one wild and precious life?

Mary Oliver, 'The Summer Day', *New and Selected Poems, Volume 1*,
Boston, MA: Beacon Press, 1992.

. . . .

WRAP HER UP IN YOUR HEART

Soon after Abi died, I received an email from one of my brides-
maids. Mandy's words provided me with the solution for what to
do with my love for Abi—where to put it, and how to go forward
with my ongoing but utterly changed relationship with her.

Through all of your pain Lucy, I know you are strong and
that you will find a way to live your life, with your darling,
beautiful, special Abi wrapped up safely in your heart where
you can take her with you wherever you go and, as you say,
love her 'always and everywhere'. I have also read your blog
and your amazing, true words about what it is to be a mother.
Death strips away all the things that are unimportant in life,
and reveals to us what is truly important in this unpredictable,
beautiful, painful world—family, friendships and love—that's all
that really counts.

More recently, I was touched by Elisabeth Kübler-Ross and
David Kessler's account of a minister who told the congregation
at a memorial service that 'you have not lost all of the things that
you loved most about your loved one. They are in you. You can
carry them with you for the rest of your life.'[7]

I will undoubtedly carry you, Abi, with me for the rest of my
life. As will all those who knew and loved you, Ella and Sally.
Wrapped up in our hearts, we will never forget your zest for life,
your enthusiasm, and we will never stop speaking your names
and sharing your stories to keep your memories alive.

I will continue to be your mum, always and forever.

Chapter 16

Post-traumatic growth

DESIGNED TO TEACH US soldiers personal resiliency skills, the Comprehensive Soldier and Family Fitness programme was described in Chapter 7. Professor Martin Seligman explained the genesis for the training programme in the *Harvard Business Review*: 'In November 2008, when the legendary General George W. Casey, Jr., the army chief of staff and former commander of the multinational force in Iraq, asked me what positive psychology had to say about soldiers' problems, I offered a simple answer: How human beings react to extreme adversity is normally distributed. On one end are the people who fall apart into PTSD (post-traumatic stress disorder), depression, and even suicide. In the middle are most people, who at first react with symptoms of depression and anxiety but within a month or so are, by physical and psychological measures, back where they were before the trauma. That is resilience. On the other end are people who show post-traumatic growth. They, too, first experience depression and anxiety, often exhibiting full-blown PTSD, but within a year they are better off than they were before the trauma. These are the people of whom Friedrich Nietzsche said, "That which does not kill us makes us stronger."[1]

During training at Westpoint, Seligman and colleagues found that 90 per cent of cadets were familiar with PTSD, but fewer than 10 per cent had heard of post-traumatic growth. This is medical illiteracy that matters, warns Seligman. 'If all a soldier knows about is PTSD, and not about resilience and growth, it creates a self-fulfilling downward spiral. Your buddy was killed yesterday in Afghanistan. Today you burst into tears and you think, "I'm falling apart; I've got PTSD; my life is ruined." These thoughts increase the symptoms of anxiety and depression—indeed PTSD is a particularly nasty combination of anxiety and depression—which in turn increases the intensity of the symptoms. Merely knowing that bursting into tears is not a symptom of PTSD, but a symptom of normal grief and mourning, usually followed by resilience, helps put the brakes on the downward spiral,' he contends.[2]

I'm not so keen on Seligman's description that the people demonstrating post-traumatic growth (PTG) were 'better off' within a year. While I realise he is referring to growth in terms of measurable scientific outcomes, the term 'better' is too easily misconstrued: as though we are casting those who don't grow as failures. But I do agree with his views on the importance of medical literacy: if we've never been told about post-traumatic growth and resilience, it's all too easy to place our symptoms as PTSD when in fact they are utterly normal and *temporary* responses to grief.

Joe Kasper, an American physician and colleague, who lost his teenage son Ryan to a rare genetic disorder, says he credits much of his recovery to the awareness of the possibility of growth after trauma, and to the awareness that positive and negative emotions are separate and distinct emotional spectrums. 'If we want to increase well-being,' he explains, 'we must clearly try to minimise misery; but in addition, we must also attempt to add positive emotion, meaning, accomplishment, and positive relationships to our lives. Given the recent advancements in positive psychology and bereavement research, and through my own experience, I now know that so much more is possible. You can grow and become a better, more complete, more empathetic and altruistic person as a result of this type of trauma. This is not to say that we should ever prescribe or wish tragedy on someone to promote growth or well-being.'[3]

Richard Tedeschi and Lawrence Calhoun, the research team behind the work on post-traumatic growth, define it as positive psychological change experienced as the direct result of the struggle with highly challenging life circumstances.[4] Richard Tedeschi is a professor of psychology at the University of North Carolina and a licensed psychologist specialising in bereavement and trauma. For the past 20 years he has led bereavement support groups, as well as publishing extensively on post-traumatic growth. Bereavement, as a highly challenging life circumstance, does present a platform for post-traumatic growth, he says. This is not to suggest that we celebrate trauma and bereavement—far from it. Rather, it is helpful to acknowledge that the worst life moments at times spark a turning point: 'It would be a misunderstanding to think that trauma is good—*we most certainly are not saying that*. What we are saying is that despite these distressing experiences, people often report positive transformations, what we have called post-traumatic growth. An important way to think about this, which has implications for clinical practice, is that the traumatic events set in motion attempts to cope and that the struggle in the *aftermath* of the trauma, *not the trauma itself*, produces the post-traumatic growth. In addition, the empirical evidence indicates that post-traumatic growth is common but certainly not universal, and as clinicians, we should never have the expectation that every trauma survivor will experience growth or that it is a necessary outcome for full trauma recovery.'[5]

Factors that contribute to post-traumatic growth

- Understanding that shattered beliefs about ourselves, others and the future are 'normal' responses to trauma.

- Being able to reduce anxiety by using techniques to control intrusive thoughts and images.

- Sharing our stories of trauma with others, rather than bottling it up (which leads to worsening physical and psychological symptoms).

- Creating a personal narrative around the trauma, which may include identifying personal strengths used, noticing how some relationships improved, or a new appreciation for life and enhanced sense of gratitude, a deepened spiritual life, and so on.

- A readiness to accept growth and develop a new life stance such as viewing oneself as more altruistic, or noticing a heightened sense of compassion.

Lisa Bucksbaum, who runs Soaringwords.com, a non-profit organisation assisting ill children and their families to heal, interviewed Richard Tedeschi in 2014. Lisa shared her interview with me for this book, but you can read more about Lisa's work online at www.soaringwords.org.

Lisa Bucksbaum (LB): When bad things happen people feel as if it will break them. Dr Tedeschi, could you explain what post-traumatic growth (PTG) is?

Richard Tedeschi (RT): In addition to the distress that comes in the aftermath of various kinds of traumatic events, people often find that they learn something of value, they change in ways that they value, they experience what might be for some a personal transformation. So this struggle, to cope and to figure out how to live with this difficulty, and the outcomes that people experience in the aftermath of these events, we call PTG.

LB: Scientists like you have been studying PTG for the past 30 years but the concept comes from ancient traditions.

RT: That's right, we've given this scientific name to it, PTG, but it's a concept that's been explored by theologians and philosophers for centuries. So you find in the great religious traditions a lot of discussion about how we should respond to suffering in our lives, they all have something to say about this aspect of human living that's inevitable. We find there's a great literature on suffering and transformation. Then when we look at philosophy, they talk about how we are inevitably going to experience some kind of suffering and trauma in our lives and how we should respond to that by trying to find some meaning despite the suffering, so we make meaningful suffering, not just suffering in vain. For example, Viktor Frankl, who was a holocaust survivor, is almost a father to this field in modern times, because he described how going through the concentration camps he found some way to make that time and that difficulty meaningful to him. So it's a purpose that developed out of that.

LB: The sense that the last freedom that one has is the freedom to choose one's attitude towards circumstances. We can't control our circumstances but we can control how we respond to them.

RT: That's exactly right. So what we've done now is try to learn about it from a scientific perspective, that is we've tried to look at what are the data that support the idea of post-traumatic growth. We've found that maybe half to two thirds of people report post-traumatic growth. It's not a universal thing but it's not uncommon—more people report post-traumatic growth than post-traumatic stress in the aftermath of various kinds of traumatic events. We're not talking about the trauma itself creating the change, we're talking about what people do in the aftermath of the trauma, about how they get through it and who can be around them that can help them make that difference so that they find something of value in it.

LB: How can other people help?

RT: Other people are really important in this process because they can help the person face up to what's happening and embrace it in some sense, by taking a look at how it's affecting you, how you are thinking about things differently now. Another person can be encouraging of that process. We want to see 'expert companionship', we want to see other people learn how to support trauma survivors in a really expert way: not expert in terms of being a professional, but someone who is a really good companion, who can listen to difficult stories, doesn't offer platitudes, but can actually learn from the person who's going through the difficulty rather than having the answers to their problems. So it's an attitude towards listening, supporting, being a presence for another person. That person who is traumatised gets a chance to articulate their experience and explain themselves—so that they can start to learn about their own way of responding to this.

In some circumstances there really aren't words, sometimes it's just knowing that someone is there and you can count on them. The expert companion is someone that stays connected to you, they don't have to be a medical practitioner, just someone who is prepared to stay with you for the long run.

During this interview, Tedeschi also identified the five different ways in which people report they've changed as a result of their reaction to trauma.

1. *A sense that they are stronger than they ever thought they could be:* Going through the traumatic event has been a great challenge, but they've found personal resources to draw upon that they weren't previously aware of.

2. *Appreciation of life:* This is the idea that people appreciate the time that we have on Earth and appreciate the things around them that they might otherwise have taken for granted.

3. *Relating to other people in a new and better way:* People report being more compassionate, empathetic and understanding,

perhaps allowing themselves to get closer to other people emotionally. Talking about traumatic events almost forces us to be more vulnerable in a way that encourages closeness.

4. *New possibilities:* Traumatic events may shut off old ideas about what's important, and usher in new priorities. New possibilities may start to open up.

5. *Spiritual change:* This encompasses a range of experiences, from religious beliefs, to existential change and the recognition of new ways of living. People may also find strength in the transformative power of nature or music.

I believe it is important to know that growth can occur from all forms of trauma, including grief. But I want to emphasise once more that growth is different from improvement and betterment. Abi's death may have led to growth, but I regard that less as self-enhancement and more as an alteration in direction. Coping with her loss has precipitated a change in perspective, a slight change in occupational priorities, and a full-frontal awareness of life's volatile and unexpected path. I'm not a better person because of it, just a different person. By covering research insights on post-traumatic growth here, I would not want to put additional pressure on any grieving person to believe that their loss has to lead to life improvement, but rather simply to know that growth is possible.

Chapter 17

Press pause

I WANT TO PRESS PAUSE for a moment—in the middle of the section on Reappraisal and Renewal—to stress how exhausting grieving is and to reiterate that it's not okay that any of us has to deal with it. I know that it is all part of life, and I've told myself time and again that death doesn't discriminate, but there are times when none of this works.

Eighteen months after Abi died, I lay in bed weeping, thinking to myself over and over again, It's not okay, it's not okay, it's not fair that Abi, Ella and Sally died and that we have to cope without them. It's not fair for them, for us or for anyone who loved them.

I'm not a slave to resilience; I hope I'm not a painfully positive fool. I certainly allow myself to succumb to my grief, to the helplessness and ongoing (although by now intermittent) misery. I often take myself off for a nap, or a walk, to hide from others in the afternoons. I can feel small, pathetic and vulnerable too. I miss Abi so much, so often and so very deeply. I hate all the good times her brothers, cousins and friends are never going to have with her—that they all would have enjoyed so much.

Even as we start to rejoin the world and find ways to relearn it, there are times when we regress. Oscillation is the norm—back and forwards we go. Don't beat yourself up over deadlines, how you think you should feel or act. There is no single way, and your way doesn't have to be my way. Grieve at your own pace and take all the rest and breaks from it you need.

THE RESILIENT GRIEVING MODEL

I have thought long and hard about the shape of my model of resilient grieving: is it a linear progression or am I moving through a cycle? In the end, I realised that, for me, grieving more resembled a jigsaw puzzle than any model containing stages to go through or tasks to be accomplished. Learning to live with grief is learning to live in a shattered world, where the familiar components have been scattered into disarray and we are left to rebuild our lives with different pieces.

Picturing the strategies I've relied upon, and covered here, as pieces of a puzzle has helped spur me on and brought some kind of order to the chaos. The pieces of the puzzle (shown overleaf) are like signposts and keys that have enabled me to navigate the ongoing process of relapse and recovery, reappraisal and renewal, acceptance and struggle, while acknowledging that this is the very nature of life.

Perhaps it is this realisation that prompts the tears that sometimes well up at someone else's loss or struggle—the overwhelming feeling of sadness that comes from knowing life is hard, and that being resilient, coping, picking up the pieces, doing it all over again is tough and tiring. It is our journey and we each have to find the pieces that fit our personal jigsaw puzzles. But we have to do it, there is no choice. We simply have to keep on going, over and over again, doing the best we can each day, each month, each year, as life comes together and falls apart, spurred on by (and savouring) the good things in our lives in a way that only the bereaved can.

The Resilient Grieving Model

(LUCY HONE, 2016)

There are no rules

Ask: Is this helping or harming?

Be realistically optimistic

Don't lose what you *have*

Accept that life is suffering

Nothing lasts forever

Trust the process

Ask: What are you hoping for now?

Resilience requires 'ordinary' magic

Choose where your focus lies

Kick the shit out of option B

Ask: What's your 'Giveaway'?

Adopt a survivor mission

Accept the good

Tell others what you need

Accept your loss

You can (and *will*) survive

Approach grief, then withdraw

Be more mindful

Use the power of distraction

Identify your secondary losses

Trauma makes you feel vulnerable

Stress: burn it off or tune it out

'Hunt the good stuff' #htgs

Develop your own 'tap code'

Remember: Other people matter

Get out and about

Exercise *is* medicine

Know your strengths and use them

Forge ongoing connections

Take a power nap

Trauma can spawn growth

Devise your own rituals

Tidy those teaspoons

Relearn the world

Chapter 18

Rituals and mourning the dead

PUBLIC MOURNING RITUALS, such as funerals, have a clear purpose. By gathering people together around the bereaved, they help mourners strengthen their bonds and re-enter the social world after a major loss. But establishing *personal rituals* to help us mourn our dead is increasingly recognised by bereavement researchers as an effective mechanism for coping better after loss.

We're not talking traditional mourning rituals here—wearing black, sitting shiva, post-funeral wakes (though these of course are vital for some)—but regular, repetitive actions that bring back memories of those who have died.

American researchers Michael Norton and Francesca Gino asked 76 research participants to write about a significant loss (the end of a relationship or the death of someone they love) and

221

to describe how they coped with that loss, including any rituals they engaged in.[1] (These researchers defined ritual as 'a symbolic activity that is performed before, during, or after a meaningful event in order to achieve some desired outcome'.) They were surprised to discover that only 10 per cent of the described rituals were performed in public; 5 per cent were performed communally, and only 5 per cent were religious in nature. Most of the rituals were therefore private, routinely practised rituals that were unique to the individual. For example, one woman who lost her mother would 'play the song by Natalie Cole "I miss you like crazy" and cry every time I heard it and thought of my mom'. One man mourning his wife wrote: 'In these fifteen years I have been going to hairdressers to cut my hair every first Saturday of the month as we used to do together.' Another widow in the study described how she washed his car every week just as her husband used to do.

THE RITUALS WE CONDUCT IN MEMORY OF THE DEAD BIND US TO THEM, THEY WORK TO MAINTAIN OUR CONNECTION WITH THEM.

When I described these type of rituals to an academic colleague, he suggested them to be painfully sad, saying he'd worry they were more likely to exacerbate depression and misery among mourners than help them heal. I was surprised by this reaction. For me, the value of rituals was immediate and obvious. The rituals we conduct in memory of the dead bind us to them, they work to maintain our connection with them and, specifically, allow us to continue to acknowledge our loss—at a specific time, place or fashion—while getting on with our 'normal' lives the rest of the time. In short, they provide something of a long-term solution, enabling us to grieve and maintain normal functioning simultaneously. They are, in essence, the answer to moving forward but retaining the dead in our lives. In this sense, I can see how they lead to the 'improved coping' found in Norton and Gino's study, but I did note on re-reading their work that they have yet to investigate the impact of rituals among people experiencing what clinicians refer to as 'complicated grief'.

Subsequent experiments by Norton and Gino have confirmed the power of rituals to mitigate grief. In a second experiment, the researchers invited 247 grieving people into their lab and had them write about their loss, describing the emotions and thoughts they experienced at the time of loss in detail.[2]

The researchers then divided participants into two groups: a 'ritual group' and a 'no-ritual group'. Participants in the ritual group were asked to write about a ritual they performed following the loss. Here, as in the previous study, many people reported private, personal and emotionally moving rituals that connected them to the memory of their lost loves in a deep and powerful way. After the writing exercise was over, the researchers measured the grief of the participants in both conditions. As one would expect, people in both groups became sad doing the exercise, but the people who wrote about rituals were *less sad*. They reported significantly less grief than those who did not write about rituals. Those in the ritual group, for example, were less inclined to endorse statements (from a standard scale used to measure grief) such as 'I feel that life is empty without this person', 'Memories of this person upset me' and 'I feel stunned or dazed over what happened'. What is interesting about this research is the discovery that the benefits of rituals accrued not only to individuals who professed a belief in rituals' effectiveness as part of the study but also to those who did not. Meaning, whether you like the idea of rituals or not, they can still help you grieve.

Norton and Gino suggest that the reason rituals help us grieve is that engaging in them helps restore a sense of control and order when we are otherwise feeling utterly powerless. Part of the magic in grieving rituals is that they are deliberately controlled gestures that help counteract the turbulence and chaos that follow loss. Crucially, these researchers also point out that rituals may not only reduce negative emotions, but also increase positive emotions.

I have developed myriad rituals since Abi, Ella and Sally died. Some of them I do regularly, some infrequently, but all of them I do to honour those we lost, and to retain their presence in our lives. I recently made a wreath out of gathered wild foliage in memory of Sally, and I frequently walk out to the local headland she loved to run on. Doing so offers me the right space and time to think of her. I will make meringues this summer using her recipe, the one the girls loved so much.

Devising rituals will be instinctive for some, but Norton and Gino's findings give encouragement for those who are not natural ritual-makers, but who might like to give it a go.

BRINGING THE BODY HOME—LEARNING FROM MĀORI GRIEVING

We are not Māori. My first encounter with one important element of Māori grieving came when my own mother died back in the year 2000 and my sister Esther suggested we bring her body home so that we would have a chance to mourn her properly before the finality of death begun. This was my first experience of seeing a dead body, and, while the concept seemed strange at first, once I was ready to spend time with her I found it beneficial. In fact, the whole experience of having my mum at home, spending time with her, not feeling rushed, and growing accustomed to seeing her dead was transformative.

Having the body of a loved one at home, or being able to view the body at a funeral home in the days following the death, provides our hearts and minds with the chance to catch up. Seeing those we loved dead seems to give us time to process the reality of our loss. Ultimately, I think it serves to place us one step further down the path of acceptance and limits denial.

We were, as I explained in Chapter 2, able to bring Abi's body home and have her there with us for five days before the funeral. It gave us the time we desperately needed to spend with her. I also think it helped the dreadful truth of her death to sink in: seeing her body there with my own eyes day after day forced my mind to acknowledge its reality, and it gave me time to reflect on her life and to dote on every last contour of her body. It helped.

Rituals to commemorate

Rituals are effective and meaningful when they have significance to the deceased and to the survivor. The following are merely suggestions and might be altered and enhanced to appropriately accommodate the relationship involved. The following list features in the *Grief Counseling Resource Guide* created by the New York State Office of Mental Health.

- Prepare a favourite meal of the loved one and enjoy it as he/she did.
- Prepare a favourite dessert—share with family or friends.
- Watch a movie(s) enjoyed by your loved one.
- Plant flowers, a tree or a flowering bush in memory of your loved one.
- Enjoy a toast to your loved one on a birthday, anniversary or holiday.
- Light a candle and recall the comfort or guiding light he/she was for you.
- Read book(s) or article(s) on a favourite topic(s) he/she enjoyed.
- Play music appreciated by your loved one and see if you can enjoy it now.
- Attend a concert/performance that would be pleasurable to you both.
- Look through photo albums and focus on shared times and memories.
- Wear a piece of jewellery that was a favourite of the person.
- Wear cologne or perfume he/she liked on you.
- Wear an item of clothing given to you by him/her.
- Buy something for yourself he/she would like you to have.

- Enjoy lunch or dinner at a favourite café/restaurant.
- Visit the burial place—bring a balloon or symbolic item to leave.
- Journal some favourite stories.
- Travel to a place he/she enjoyed or always wanted to visit.
- Review how your life is better because he/she was a part of it.
- Focus on the gift he/she was to you.
- Purchase flowers on the anniversary. Bring for display at church or a home gathering. When people leave, have them take a flower.
- Send flowers to a close family member on the anniversary.
- Read a favourite poem(s) or book enjoyed by your loved one.
- Watch home videos and remember.
- Volunteer for an organisation in memory of your loved one.
- Become an activist in the cause of death issue—by participating in a walk-a-thon, phone-a-thon, etc.
- If you kept greeting cards given to you by your loved one, take time to read them again.
- Enjoy a leisurely walk, taking time to recall shared events in life together.[3]

JAN STANLEY'S RITUALS FOR GRIEVING

Since 1999, American leadership consultant Jan Stanley has lost her parents, her best friend and sister, making her the only member of her family of origin still alive. Jan has found rituals helpful in her own grieving process, which subsequently resulted in more and more friends and acquaintances asking for her assistance in designing rituals. She has described some of the rituals she has used for her own grief and those she has since devised at the request of others.

1. Writing a eulogy

Writing a eulogy is a ritual in a certain way. When we pour our hearts into the writing of a tribute, it helps us to remember the person we loved and also opens the door for our healing to truly begin. A beautiful ritualistic approach to eulogy writing is to collect stories and memories from those who knew the person well and weave them into a sketch of the person's life. I always say that a good eulogy honours the person who died and uplifts all those who hear it. A good eulogy makes us want to be better people.

2. Giving away meaningful possessions

This ritual comes to me from a Native American ceremony that I attended about 10 years ago. A member of the community had been killed in a motorcycle accident. Elders did a ceremonial dance to create sacred space on a big field and then the wife took meaningful possessions from her deceased husband and gave them to the person who she felt would be the best keeper—putting them to good use. I have since used this giving away ritual after my Mum died and after my sister died. I also encourage others to use it, too. The giving away is a way to ensure that the essence of the person—their ideals, their hobbies, their values—lives on.

3. Washing my sister/preparing the body

This ritual is coming back some 100 years after it was common-place due to a resurgence of dying at home and home funerals.

When my sister died in her home in 2013, one of her daughters and I tenderly cleaned her body in preparation for her funeral. We also covered her in a prayer shawl that her daughters had made and then a lace coverlet that my daughter and I had purchased at an antique shop. This is a ritual for saying goodbye to the body that our loved one inhabited.

4. Carrying on a favourite tradition

The day my sister died, we all decided to go to the annual Fourth of July (American Independence Day) celebration that night in her honour, as it was one of her favourite holidays. In a similar way, I always buy a geranium on Mother's Day, a tradition I carry on each year. I know daughters who continue to make a special recipe of sauerkraut with an old fashioned cabbage slicing tool to honour their father's tradition; a husband whose wife had always corresponded with family members carried on the tradition of sending Christmas cards to all family and friends; a friend who carried a horrible tasting liqueur in his golf bag and drank a toast while golfing to carry on the tradition of his lifelong friend.

5. Calling on/remembering a loved one for inspiration

A client was struggling with low energy and fatigue after the death of her sister. We created a morning and evening ritual for her using a necklace that had been given to her by her sister. She used the necklace to summon her strength and courage—traits that she knew her deceased sibling would want her to carry on. She says it helps her feel her sister's presence.

More of Jan Stanley's suggestions for Good Life Rituals can be found at www.goodliferituals.com.

Chapter 19

Nothing lasts forever

ULTIMATELY, BEREAVEMENT IS JUST another part of life, because nothing and no one lasts forever. To deny that is to deny being human.

I love British chat-show host Graham Norton's thoughts on forever, written at the end of his most recent book, *The Life and Loves of a He Devil*. 'Who came up with this concept that's designed to torture and disappoint us? Nothing lasts for ever and that's just the way things should be.' He goes on to explain that, however much he loves Bailey (his current dog), he knows their time together is limited, as, like all living things, Bailey too will eventually die.

'Of course if I was asked if I wanted Bailey to live for ever I would say yes, but in reality knowing that he will leave me makes my time with him more precious, the love bittersweet.'[1]

His advice to 'enjoy the party because we know there will come a time when the music will be switched off and the lights switched on' appeals to me. Actually, it does more than that: it hones in on a fundamental truth that guides my life, and, I've come to realise, has guided my grieving. 'One of the great joys of life,' he writes, 'is knowing that things change. Relish the happy times; endure the sad. For ever is a pointless fantasy. Everything comes to an end.'

We have to accept that we will be faced with myriad losses during our lives. We know that rationally, but I now think that grasping this truism—accepting that death is universally part of life—actually helps us to live better as well as to grieve better. It has motivated me to pull myself out of the dark hole of my grief and return to the living, to be present and grateful for all that I have and can do. Not tomorrow but just for today.

Viewing death as inevitable puts us back in touch with our natural life cycle: we are born, we live, we may raise a family, achieve things, love, but we all eventually die. That is the human life course. Our time on this planet is short. Make it count.

Chapter 20

A final word

I HAVE ONE LAST THING to say on the matter of grief—and what losing Abi has taught us.

I suspect that our grieving experience has, in part, been made a great deal easier by the fact that we know Abi had a good life. Her twelve short years were packed full of living, she was profoundly loved and (this is the crucial bit) she knew it. Little Abi Hone knew that her parents loved her, her brothers loved her, her wider family loved her, friends loved her, and all her school teachers and community did too. In that respect she led a charmed life.

We often hear the bereaved long for 'just one more minute' or 'just one more chance' but one more minute holds little appeal for me. One more minute is no use at all: it is the decades of her life I long for.

I've pondered this over the past months and decided that, at the core of our ability to accept her loss and endure life without her, lies a lack of regret. We have no need of one more minute with Abi because we have nothing more to say. We said it all while she was here, straight to her face, while she was living. Through thought and word and deed—and texts, emails and voice messages, Instagram, Facebook and Snapchat too. We watched movies, read books, baked cakes, collected shells, swam, sang, laughed and cried.

We didn't say goodbye to her on that last day. The last time we saw her alive she jumped out of the car and ran off to the netball courts to watch Ella's team play. But that doesn't matter either, because we'd said goodbye so many times before (and hello, I love you and sleep tight). That single absence means nothing in a lifetime of presence.

Because she knew she was loved and we'd done so much with her, we have nothing to regret. Ultimately, that is the essence to living and dying: to do it all and say it all while those you care for are still here. That is my message for the living. So, even if, sadly, it is too late to tell these things to the person you are grieving today, there's always someone else out there who needs to hear it. Say it, do it, no regrets.

We know we will never get over the loss of our little girl. Instead, life grows around her absence and we are learning to carry that pain. We were lucky to have her for the short years she lived.

We will always have you, dear Abi, wrapped up in our hearts.

We will never stop loving you.

Always and forever.

HE SLEEPS IN A STORM

At Abi's funeral our good friend and chaplain, Jimmy Ullrich, shared the following parable with us. Actually, he said it was a true story, from Mitch Albom's newest book, *Have a Little Faith* (Albom also wrote *Tuesdays with Morrie*, which I loved). Apparently, this story was first recounted in a sermon, back in 1975 by Albom's Rabbi.

A man seeks employment on a farm. He hands his letter of recommendation to his employer. It reads simply, 'He sleeps in a storm.'

The owner is desperate for help, so he hires the man.

Several weeks pass, and suddenly, in the middle of the night, a powerful storm rips through the valley.

Awakened by the swirling rain and howling wind, the owner leaps out of the bed. He calls for his new hired hand, but the man is sleeping soundly.

So he dashes off to the barn. He sees, to his amazement, that the animals are secure with plenty of feed.

He runs out to the field. He sees the bales of wheat have been bound and are wrapped in tarpaulins.

He races to the silo. The doors are latched, and the grain is dry.

And then he understands, 'He sleeps in a storm.'

My friends, if we tend to the things that are important in life, if we are right with those we love and behave in line with our faith, our lives will not be cursed with the aching throb of unfulfilled business. Our words will always be sincere, our embraces tight. We will never wallow in the agony of 'I could have, I should have.' We can sleep in a storm.

And when it's time, our good-byes will be complete.

M. Albom, *Have a Little Faith*, London: Hachette Digital, 2009, p. 93.

Notes

Chapter 1

1 This quote has most frequently been attributed to Ralph Waldo Emerson, but is more likely to be taken from a 1905 essay by Bessie A. Stanley.
2 A. Masten, 'Ordinary magic', *American Psychologist*, 2001, 56(3), p. 227.
3 V. Frankl, *Man's Search for Meaning*, New York, NY: Simon & Schuster, 1959, p. 23.
4 Skylight, *When You're Grieving: Some helpful info and ideas to help you on the journey*, Wellington, NZ: Skylight Trust, 2009.
5 E. Kübler-Ross, *On Death and Dying*, New York, NY: Routledge, 1973.
6 Frankl, p. 66.
7 While I was introduced to this poem as 'She Is Gone', its official title is 'Remember Me'. It was used by Queen Elizabeth II at the funeral for the Queen Mother and credited 'anonymous'. For the full and fascinating story on its provenance and how the true author was discovered, see www.poeticexpressions.co.uk/poems/you%20can%20shed%20tears%20that%20she%20is%20gone.htm

Chapter 2

1 M. Csikszentmihalyi, *Flow: The psychology of optimal experience*, New York, NY: Harper Collins, 1990, p. 29.
2 Csikszentmihalyi, p. 30.

3 S. Fox, *Creating a New Normal . . . After the death of a child*, Bloomington, NY: iUniverse Inc., 2010, p. 41.
4 Csikszentmihalyi, p. 33.
5 K. Reivich, personal communication, 7 July 2014.
6 K. Mossman, personal communication, 10 July 2014.
7 P. Chödrön, *When Things Fall Apart: Heart advice for difficult times*, Boston, MA: Shambhala Publications, 2005, pp. 10, 15.
8 Chödrön, p. 13.
9 W. Worden, *Grief Counseling and Grief Therapy: A handbook for the mental health practitioner*, 4th edn, New York, NY: Springer Publishing, 2009, p. 44.
10 B. Noel and P. Blair, *I Wasn't Ready to Say Goodbye: Surviving, coping and healing after the sudden death of a loved one*, Naperville, IL: Sourcebooks, 2008.

Chapter 3

1 R. Newman, 'Resilience and psychology: A healthy relationship', 2003, www.apa.org/monitor/julaug03/pp.aspx (accessed 14 January 2016).
2 S. Southwick, 'The Science of Resilience', www.huffingtonpost.com/ steven-m-southwick/trauma-resilience_b_1881666.html (accessed 26 February 2016).
3 D. Charney, 'Resilience: The science of mastering life's greatest challenges', online lecture for the Brain & Behavior Research Foundation, recorded on 9 July 2013 (accessed 25 October 2015), see www.youtube.com/ watch?v=AEWnTjgGVcw
4 K. Reivich, personal communication, 7 July 2014.
5 T. Attig, 'Interview with Tom Attig', www.griefsheart.com/tominterview. php (accessed 14 January 2016).
6 G.A. Bonanno, *The Other Side of Sadness: What the new science of bereavement tells us about life after loss*, New York, NY: Basic Books, 2009, p. 76.
7 Bonanno, *The Other Side of Sadness*, p. 20.
8 G.A. Bonanno, 'Loss, trauma, and human resilience: Have we underestimated the human capacity to thrive after extremely aversive events?', *American Psychologist*, 2004, 59(1), p. 21.
9 Bonanno, 'Loss, trauma, and human resilience', p. 21.
10 G.A. Bonanno and S. Kaltman, 'The varieties of grief experience', *Clinical Psychology Review*, 2001, 21, pp. 705–34.
11 Bonanno, 'Loss, trauma, and human resilience', p. 23.
12 A.D. Mancini, G.A. Bonanno and A.E. Clark, 'Stepping off the hedonic treadmill: Latent class analyses of individual differences in response to major life events', *Journal of Individual Differences*, 2011, 32(3), pp. 144–52.
13 D. Charney, 'The Resilience Prescription', www.mountsinai.org/static_files/ MSMC/Files/Patient%20Care/Occupational%20Health/Resilience PrescriptionPromotion-082112.pdf (accessed 5 December 2015).

Chapter 4

1 T. Attig, *How We Grieve: Relearning the world*, rev. edn, New York, NY: Oxford University Press, 2011, p. xxxv.

Chapter 5

1 G.A. Bonanno, *The Other Side of Sadness: What the new science of bereavement tells us about life after loss*, New York, NY: Basic Books, 2009, p. 7.
2 S. Fox, *Creating a New Normal . . . After the death of a child*, Bloomington, NY: iUniverse Inc., 2010, p. 37.
3 W. Martin, *Primates of Park Avenue: A memoir*, New York, NY: Simon & Schuster, 2015, p. 198.
4 M. Gurven and H. Kaplan, 'Longevity among hunter-gatherers: A cross-cultural examination', *Population and Development Review*, 2007, 33(2), pp. 321–65.
5 Martin, p. 205.
6 Martin, p. 205.
7 Bonanno, p. 47.
8 T. Attig, *How We Grieve: Relearning the world*, rev. edn, New York, NY: Oxford University Press, 2011, p. xxvii.
9 Attig, p. xxx.
10 Attig, p. xxxi.

Chapter 6

1 E. Kübler-Ross and D. Kessler, *On Grief & Grieving: Finding the meaning of grief through the five stages of loss*, New York, NY: Scribner, 2014, p. 76.
2 W. Martin, *Primates of Park Avenue: A Memoir*, New York, NY: Simon & Schuster, 2015, p. 219.
3 The Dalai Lama, H.H., 'Foreword', in *The Tibetan Book of the Dead*, New York, NY: Bantam, 1994, p. xvii.
4 G.A. Bonanno, C. Wortman, D. Lehman et al., 'Resilience to loss and chronic grief: A prospective study from preloss to 18 months postloss', *Journal of Personality and Social Psychology*, 2002, 83(5), pp. 1150–64.
5 G.A. Bonanno, *The Other Side of Sadness: What the new science of bereavement tells us about life after loss*, New York, NY: Basic Books, 2009, p. 128.

Chapter 7

1 A.D. Ong, C.S. Bergeman and S.M. Boker, 'Resilience comes of age: Defining features in later adulthood', *Journal of Personality*, 2009, 77(6), pp. 1777–804.
2 R.S. Lazarus, A.D. Kanner and S. Folkman, 'A cognitive-phenomenological analysis', in R. Plutchik and H. Kellerman (eds), *Theories of Emotion*, New York, NY: Academic Press, 1980, pp. 189–217.
3 B.L. Fredrickson, K.A. Coffey and J. Pek et al., 'Open hearts build lives: Positive emotions, induced through loving-kindness meditation, build consequential personal resources', *Journal of Personality and Social Psychology*, 2008, 95(5), pp. 1045–62.
4 S. Lyubomirsky, L. King and E. Diener, 'The benefits of frequent positive affect: Does happiness lead to success?' *Psychological Bulletin*, 2005, 131(6), pp. 803–55.

5   B.L. Fredrickson, *Positivity: Groundbreaking research reveals how to embrace the hidden strength of positive emotions, overcome negativity, and thrive*, New York, NY: Crown Publishers, 2009, pp. 99, 101.

6   B.L. Fredrickson, M.M. Tugade, C.E. Waugh and G.R. Larkin, 'What good are positive emotions in crises?: A prospective study of resilience and emotions following the terrorist attacks on the United States on September 11, 2001', *Journal of Personality and Social Psychology*, 2003, 84(2), pp. 365–76.

7   Fredrickson, *Positivity*, p. 102.

8   G.A. Bonanno, S. Galea, A. Bucciarelli and D. Vlahov, 'Psychological resilience after disaster: New York City in the aftermath of the September 11th terrorist attack', *Psychological Science*, 2006, 17(3), pp. 181–6.

9   A.D. Ong, C.S. Bergeman, T.L. Bisconti and K.A. Wallace, 'Psychological resilience, positive emotions, and successful adaptation to stress in later life', *Journal of Personality and Social Psychology*, 2006, 91(4), pp. 730–49.

10 Ong, Bergeman and Boker, 'Resilience comes of age', pp. 1777–804.

11 K. Britton, 'Grief is part of life', blog written for *Positive Psychology News Daily*, 26 May 2011, http://positivepsychologynews.com/news/kathryn-britton/2011052617816 (accessed 20 October 2015).

12 T. Ben-Shahar, 'Five ways to become happier today', recorded 23 September 2009, http://bigthink.com/videos/five-ways-to-become-happier-today (accessed 23 February 2016).

13 E. O'Brien, personal communication, 10 November 2015.

14 G.A. Bonanno, *The Other Side of Sadness: What the new science of bereavement tells us about life after loss*, New York, NY: Basic Books, 2009, p. 30.

15 C. Wortman, 'Positive emotions: Do they have a role in the grieving process?' blog written for This Emotional Life, www.pbs.org/thisemotion-allife/blogs/positive-emotions-do-they-have-role-grieving-process (accessed 4 November 2015).

16 See www.griefsheart.com.

17 D. Charney, 'Resilience: The science of mastering life's greatest challenges', online lecture for the Brain & Behavior Research Foundation, 9 July 2013, www.youtube.com/watch?v=AEWnTjgGVcw (accessed 26 February 2016).

18 D. Keltner and G.A. Bonanno, 'A study of laughter and dissociation: Distinct correlates of laughter and smiling during bereavement', *Journal of Personality and Social Psychology*, 1997, 73(4), pp. 687–702.

19 F. Bryant, 'Savoring Beliefs Inventory (SBI): A scale for measuring beliefs about savoring', *Journal of Mental Health*, 2003, 12(2), pp. 175–96.

Chapter 8

1   M. Stroebe and H. Schut, 'The dual process model of coping with bereavement: Rationale and description', *Death Studies*, 1999, 23(3), pp. 197–224.

2   Stroebe and Schut, p. 216.

3   C. Rushton, personal communication, 1 December 2015.

4   Stroebe and Schut, p. 216.

5   C. Wortman, personal communication, 19 January 2016.

6   C. Wortman, 'Positive emotions: Do they have a role in the grieving process?' blog written for This Emotional Life, www.pbs.org/

thisemotionallife/blogs/positive-emotions-do-they-have-role-grieving-process (accessed 4 November 2015).

7 Stroebe and Schut.

8 www.bbc.co.uk/radio4/features/desert-island-discs/find-a-castaway

Chapter 9

1 K. Reivich and A. Shatté, *The Resilience Factor: 7 keys to finding your inner strength and overcoming life's hurdles*, New York, NY: Broadway Books, 2002, p. 43.

2 S. Ahmad, A. Feder and E.J. Lee, 'Earthquake impact in a remote South Asian population: Psychosocial factors and posttraumatic symptoms', *Journal of Traumatic Stress*, 2010, 23(3), pp. 408–12.

3 www.1wildandpreciouslife.com/2015/03/the-universal-law-of-impermanence/

4 Reivich and Shatté, p. 43.

5 C.S. Lewis, *A Grief Observed*, London: Faber & Faber, 1961, p. 9.

6 J.S. Cheavens, D.B. Feldman and A. Gum, 'Hope therapy in a community sample: A pilot investigation', *Social Indicators Research*, 2006, 77(1), pp. 61–78.

7 J. Kabat-Zinn, 'Mindfulness-based interventions in context: Past, present, and future', *Clinical Psychology: Science and practice*, 2003, 10(2): pp. 144–56.

8 Kabat-Zinn.

9 J. Cacciatore and M. Flint, 'ATTEND: Toward a mindfulness-based bereavement care model', *Death Studies*, 2012, 36(1): pp. 61–82.

Chapter 10

1 For a review of resilience research among children and youth, see A. Masten, 'Global perspectives on resilience in children and youth', *Child Development*, 2014, 85(1), pp. 6–20.

2 D. Charney, 'Resilience: The science of mastering life's greatest challenges', online lecture for the Brain & Behavior Research Foundation, recorded 9 July 2013, www.youtube.com/watch?v=AEWnTjgGVcw (accessed 25 October 2015).

3 National Scientific Council on the Developing Child, 'Supportive relation-ships and active-skill-building strengths: The foundations of resilience', Working Paper 13, 2015.

4 Charney.

5 T.L. Bisconti, C.S. Bergeman and S.M. Boker, 'Social support as a predictor of variability: An examination of the adjustment trajectories of recent widows', *Psychology and Aging*, 2006, 21, pp. 590–9.

6 A. Schweitzer, *The Light Within Us*, New York, NY: Philosophical Library, 1959.

7 S. Fox, *Creating a New Normal . . . After the death of a child*, Bloomington, NY: iUniverse Inc., 2010.

8 S. Sandberg, Facebook post, 4 June 2015.

9 J. Gross, 'Farewell to my daughter Kate, who died on Christmas day', January 2015, www.theguardian.com/lifeandstyle/2015/jan/10/

farewell-to-my-daughter-kate-who-died-on-christmas-day (accessed 26 February 2016).

10 Interview with T. Attig from his website, www.griefsheart.com/tominter-view.php (accessed 26 February 2016).

11 E. Kübler-Ross and D. Kessler, *On Grief & Grieving: Finding the meaning of grief through the five stages of loss*, New York, NY: Scribner, 2014, p. 66.

12 W.J. Worden, *Grief Counseling and Grief Therapy: A handbook for the mental health professional*, 3rd edn, New York, NY: Springer Publications, 2002.

13 R. Moran, 'Just Say You Are Sorry', 1999, originally published in *The Compassionate Friend* newsletter, Fort Lauderdale, FL.

14 T. Lawrence, Everything Doesn't Happen For a Reason, blog post, 20 October 2015, see www.timjlawrence.com/blog/2015/10/19/everything-doesnt-happen-for-a-reason (accessed 23 February 2016).

Chapter 11

1 For a comprehensive list and access to these studies, see www.viacharacter.org/www/Research/Character-Research-Findings.

2 N. Park, C. Peterson and M.E. Seligman, 'Strengths of character and well-being', *Journal of Social and Clinical Psychology*, 2004, 23(5), pp. 603–19.

3 T.N. Alim, A. Feder, R.E. Graves et al., 'Trauma, resilience, and recovery in a high-risk African-American population', *American Journal of Psychiatry*, 2008, 165(12), pp. 1566–75.

4 E. O'Brien, personal communication, 10 November 2015.

5 T. Rashid and A. Anjum, '340 Ways to Use VIA Character Strengths', University of Pennsylvania, 2005, http://tayyabrashid.com/pdf/via_strengths.pdf (accessed 26 February 2016).

6 D. Charney, 'Resilience: The science of mastering life's greatest challenges', online lecture for the Brain & Behavior Research Foundation, 9 July 2013, www.youtube.com/watch?v=AEWnTjgGVcw (accessed 25 October 2015).

Chapter 12

1 T. Ben-Shahar, *Choose the Life You Want: The mindful way to happiness*, reprint edn, New York, NY: The Experiment, 2014; *Happier: Learn the secrets to daily joy and lasting fulfillment*, New York, NY: McGraw-Hill Professional, 2007; *The Pursuit of Perfect: How to stop chasing perfection and start living a richer, happier life*, New York, NY: McGraw-Hill, 2009.

2 For a short summary of the lifestyle habits that contribute to depression and a prescription for avoidance, watch S. Ilardi's TED talk, www.youtube.com/watch?v=drv3BP0Fdi8 (accessed 26 February 2016).

3 T. Ben-Shahar, 'Five Ways to Become Happier Today', recorded 23 September 2009, http://bigthink.com/videos/five-ways-to-become-happier-today (accessed 23 February 2016).

4 S. Ilardi, *The Depression Cure*, London: Vermillion, 2010, p. viii.

5 J.J. Ratey, *Spark: The revolutionary new science of exercise and the brain*, New York, NY: Little, Brown & Company, 2008.

6 Ilardi, p. 16.

7 Ilardi, p. 131.

8 J. Prochaska, C. Redding and K. Evers, 'The transtheoretical model and stages of change', in K. Glanz, F. Lewis and B. Rimer (eds), *Health Behavior and Health Education*, San Francisco, CA: Jossey-Bass, 1997, pp. 60–84.
9 J. Prochaska, J. Norcross and C. Diclemente, 'Applying the stages of change', *Psychotherapy in Australia* 2013, (19)2, p. 4.
10 E. O'Brien, personal communication, 10 November 2015.

Chapter 13

1 R. Neimeyer, *The Lessons of Loss: A guide to coping*, New York, NY: McGraw-Hill, 1998.
2 G.A. Bonanno, *The Other Side of Sadness: What the new science of bereavement tells us about life after loss*, New York, NY: Basic Books, 2009, p. 8.
3 T. Attig, *How We Grieve: Relearning the world*, rev. edn, New York, NY: Oxford University Press, 2011, p. xl.
4 C.G. Davis, S. Nolen-Hoeksema and J. Larson, 'Making sense of loss and benefiting from the experience: Two construals of meaning', *Journal of Personality and Social Psychology*, 72(2), pp. 561–74.
5 A. Assad, personal communication, 30 October 2015.

Chapter 14

1 Adapted from S. Sandberg's Facebook post, 4 June 2015, www.facebook.com/sheryl/posts/10155617891025177:0 (accessed 12 October 2015).
2 M. Warrington, personal communication, 19 November 2015.
3 J. Kasper, 'Co-destiny: A conceptual goal for parental bereavement and the call for a "positive turn" in the scientific study of the parental bereavement process', Capstone thesis, University of Pennsylvania, 1 August 2013.
4 R.N. Remen MD, blog post, 'Walking the Path', 19 August 2015, www.rachelremen.com/walking-the-path/ (accessed 13 October 2015).

Chapter 15

1 G.A. Bonanno, *The Other Side of Sadness: What the new science of bereavement tells us about life after loss*, New York, NY: Basic Books, 2009, p. 72.
2 T. Attig, *How We Grieve: Relearning the world*, rev. edn, New York, NY: Oxford University Press, 2011, p. 189.
3 For a comprehensive review of this literature, see B.L. Root and J.J. Exline, 'The role of continuing bonds in coping with grief: Overview and future directions', *Death Studies*, 2014, 38, pp. 1–8.
4 W.J. Worden, *Grief Counseling and Grief Therapy: A handbook for the mental health professional*, 3rd edn, New York, NY: Springer Publications, 2002, p. 50.
5 D. Quinlan, personal communication, 20 October 2015.
6 Bonanno, p. 73.
7 E. Kübler-Ross and D. Kessler, *On Grief & Grieving: Finding the meaning of grief through the five stages of loss*, New York, NY: Scribner, 2014, p. 61.

Chapter 16

1 M.E. Seligman, 'Building resilience', *Harvard Business Review*, 89(4), 2011, pp. 100–6.

2 M.E. Seligman, *Flourish: A visionary new understanding of happiness and well-being*, New York, NY: Free Press, 2011, pp. xii, 349.
3 J. Kasper, 'Co-destiny: A conceptual goal for parental bereavement and the call for a "positive turn" in the scientific study of the parental bereavement process', Capstone thesis, University of Pennsylvania, 1 August 2013.
4 R.G. Tedeschi and L.G. Calhoun, 'Posttraumatic growth: Conceptual foundations and empirical evidence', *Psychological Inquiry*, 2004, 15(1), pp. 1–18.
5 R.G. Tedeschi and L.G. Calhoun, 'A clinical approach to posttraumatic growth', in A. Linley and K.S. Joseph (eds), *Positive Psychology in Practice*, Hoboken, NJ: John Wiley & Sons, 2004.

Chapter 18

1 M.I. Norton and F. Gino, 'Rituals alleviate grieving for loved ones, lovers, and lotteries', *Journal of Experimental Psychology: General*, 2014, 143(1), pp. 266–72.
2 Norton and Gino, p. 267.
3 S. Wheeler-Roy and B.A. Amyot, *Grief Counseling Resource Guide: A field manual*, New York, NY: New York State Office of Mental Health, 2004.

Chapter 19

1 G. Norton, *The Life and Loves of a He Devil: A memoir*, London: Hodder & Stoughton, 2014, p. 287.